IN SEARCH OF BEING
Man in Conflict with the Spectre of Nothingness

IN SEARCH OF BEING
Man in Conflict
with the
Spectre of Nothingness

Manoel Joaquim de Carvalho, Jr.

Philosophical Library
New York

Library of Congress Cataloging in Publication Data $8-85$

Carvalho Júnior, Manoel Joaquim de.
   In search of being.

   1. Ontology.   2. Existentialism.   I. Title.
BD331.C363   1984   111   84-19079
ISBN 0-8022-2424-5

An abridged version of this work has been published in German as AUF DER SUCHE NACH DEM SEIN (Strom-Verlag, Zurich, 1976). Abridged and translated into French by Rev. Blaise Pons. Translated into English by Susan Wald.

Table of Contents

Being and Consciousness of Self

From Consciousness of Existence
to the Depths of Being

The human being newly arrived in the world may lack the mental development sufficient for reasoning, but he nevertheless has an innate consciousness of something that both dominates and defines him; he knows, he feels that he exists. This consciousness of himself is not necessarily a knowledge of his ego. He does not need to explore the inner sanctum of his personality or the depths of his being. This intuition requires no great intellectual effort. However, it gives him a very clear certainty of two things: that he exists, and that he does so as his own irreplaceable entity for which no one else can substitute.

Even in the act of forming a couple, where we really see the fusion of two bodies and two souls into a single living reality, even the most complete union of desires, thoughts, and actions cannot erase that idea which is as old as man himself: the human being exists in himself and by himself.

There are intensely felt moments in which this consciousness is particularly vivid—when the instinct of self-preservation comes into play; when one feels the greatest joys and when one is in ecstasy or has a powerful dream. Likewise, the desire for possession stirs up strong feelings of individuality in everyone.

1

But it is artistic creation that gives rise to the strongest feelings of singleness. Poets, musicians, and inventors know that the work they have created stems from their own personality. Even more than the results of mental labor, creative achievements are the product of an existence and a life. The consciousness of existing is redoubled in view of what has sprung from the depths of an individuality. And this super consciousness stemming from the use of creative abilities calls forth a new super consciousness, which is inseparable from the love for a created object.

Yet even aside from such moments of special consciousness of his ego, the human being never loses the consciousness of being himself. However small his thinking capacity, however limited his means of expression, something remains in him that allows him to escape the animal condition. No amount of "brainwashing" can prevent a person from recognizing himself. Even in states of semiconsciousness he retains instinctive reactions that bear the indelible mark of his ego, the certainty that it is he, and not someone else, who is faced with the good or bad events of his life.

As for suffering, unlike and like happy moments, it is a stimulus of individual consciousness. It may even be said that pain opens the gates of being for everyone. A person who suffers descends more deeply than others into the depths of human reality. His own torments may destroy the existential framework of his life: inherited tendencies and acquired habits. And on that razed foundation he can build a structure that is much more personal, built according to his exact wishes, but which is also much more universal, appearing in a purer, brighter light. This is equally true of physical suffering, which includes the awareness of gnawing pain and of the being itself which is gnawed by it, and of moral suffering, which prepares the mind to accept the truth beyond what Dante called the "wilderness" of life.

Yet the acceptance of truth is already a superhuman act, divine in essence. It is made possible by human suffering; that is what the myth of young Demophon aims to show. In order to be accepted as one of the gods, he had to lie down three times without crying on a bed of hot coals prepared by Demeter. But though he passed the test, his mother Metanira refused to allow his apotheosis; she wanted him to remain mortal and imperfect. Thus, the human soul is blocked in its desire to take flight; it is condemned to suffering, the purpose of which is to make it divine, but not to permit it, in the final analysis, to escape the tragedy of existence, that tragedy expressed by Dante.

Shakespeare also, to some extent, expressed it in his formula "To be or not to be." Concise as it may be, this phrase raises a much broader question than the psychological awareness of self which any primitive person or child innately possesses. It raises the question of eternity. For the fact of our existence establishes itself in our mind, but thereby makes us conscious of our reality as an immortal being, as "spirit." This divine gift partakes of the divine essence, and therefore will not disappear. In becoming conscious that he lives in time, man has the revelation that he will still be living when time itself— that creation of his mind—has gone by. And the consciousness of his being will survive as well, along with his being.

The brilliant thing about Hamlet's phrase is the statement that one cannot be and not be simultaneously. If a person *is*, nothing can make him become *nothing*. If he exists, he cannot, at the same time, not exist. Essence and existence are given to us, and cannot be refused. Spinoza said: "*Essentia involvit existentiam*." But this gift, according to Kierkegaard, can come only from God, i.e., from the Existence that *is* Essence.

These formulas make consciousness of self eternal; Hegel's makes it universal: "Consciousness of self is something only insofar as it becomes foreign to itself; in this way it can be represented as universal; but that universality which belongs to it is its subjective value and its effectiveness." It should be added that the consciousness of existing is not unique to man, but is common to all individuals. Man experiences himself as a being even if he does not know that this is universal, and even if he learns it only after the fact.

Another of Hegel's formulas is that "the self of consciousness is the Being." Two different interpretations may be made of it: that being is the basis of consciousness, or that consciousness of self is confused with being itself. In reality, being and consciousness blend in man like two notes in a chord. No one can "be" without being conscious of being.

But the dual consciousness of being and of existing is in fact a challenge to nothingness. Bergson saw that the notion of nothingness was a creation of the mind, something constructed to serve as an antithesis of being, not a reality that precedes it. Man however, could imagine it only *as a result* of his full consciousness of being and of existing. What is nothingness to a plant? And what is nothingness to an animal, which has no intellective existence? We should add that, despite Hegel's formula, this lack of intellective existence preents an animal from aspiring to essence, though it may live and exist. In man, on the other hand, essence and existence complement one another. Existentialism, by refusing to pose the problem of being, has ignored what gives meaning to that which is human.

Another possible image of the relationship between essence and existence is that of the fire and the flames. These are two inseparable realities; one is a function of the other, and yet they can be distinguished. The consciousness of existing is not essence itself, but it reveals to man what he is.

The Being is that which *is*. And the human being is in His image. The human being's consciousness stems from his being, and shows him both that he exists and that he "*is*." Descartes' "cogito,", like Berdyaev's reply to it ("I think, therefore I 'exist' ") both err in not simultaneously affirming both realities.

If the essence-being could not exist, it would not be human. But if the existence-being lacked essence, it would not go beyond the vegetal stage.

Finally, why not approach the problem of the relation between essence and existence as that of the relationship between the soul and the body? For the consciousness of existing, which unites the two components of being, is a gift of God, exactly like the human soul. What would a man be without a soul? No myth, however bold, has ever dared to portray a monster such as the modern world is thinking of creating.

But man's life is only a journey toward truth. It has no meaning other than to lead to a certain kind of knowledge of the Creator: not in His supreme existence, but in contemplating it from the threshold.

It is only through contemplating his own being—his essence and his existence—that man finds a way to go beyond his own reality. It is as though his eyes rested on a vast panorama, which opened to a light making it still more majestic.

Being and Consciousness of Self

1. *The search for oneself*

The Being is essentially a search. It is a search for oneself, for this method, which gives proof of the Being and gives it value, may be considered as being itself. The human being who introspects according to this method of self-construction develops into an integral person. This intimate monologue builds a strength in him that can make him a winner of the struggle in the world. The principal cause of the reigning instability in modern society is the value placed on existence at the expense of essence, of which only a deepened consciousness can prevent man's self-destruction by means of his scientific discoveries.

This development is proportional to the effort each person makes, but only the edge of the abyss can be reached, for man will never get to the bottom of himself. His search is difficult, for he himself is its goal.

Man represents a universe made unintelligible by its vastness, like the cosmos itself. Yet despite this, he is the only creature with the hope of penetrating to the depths of being, provided he can gain insight into his inner life. This is not possible without sacrifice; the search for self and emotion, for example, are opposite methods—

5

while the latter rises to the surface, the former descends to the bottom.

But this descent toward the bottomless depths responds to a voice that cries within us but remains unanswered: a cry that is the very essence of being, a chase in which the hunter and the prey are one. Both are a proof that the Being "*is*" in a perfect way.

In any case, the Being must not be considered as cut off from its potentiality, nor defined only as "being-as-a-being." The *Esse* (that which is) has a meaning. The search for this meaning has proceeded clumsily; it was not enough to guess that the meaning existed. Man is like a temple of which the roof must be destroyed in order to view the interior. The meaning of the word "being" is in its inner profundity.

There is no search without a goal. But the search for being is disconcerting, for the goal and the seeker are one. Unable to detach himself from himself, man loses himself in the inner recesses of his being. His exploration becomes an entreaty. But there is only one answer, that of the Creator, and it is imperceptible: only consciousness can intercept that voice.

Dialogue is possible then, between the finite being and the infinite Being. But despite Heidegger's statement, it is not nothingness which speaks. Can nothingness have a voice?

2. *Human trinity*

Human reality constitutes a perfect trinity—essence, existence, and consciousness. Like the particles of an atom, they cannot be separated without destroying the whole. But contemporary existentialists and psychoanalysts run the risk of doing precisely that: do not Heidegger and Sartre assail the notion of essence, and Freud the notion of consciousness?

Unlike the animals, a man is capable of consciousness as well as knowledge of himself, which is the fundamental expression of his being. Spinoza stated "*Essentia involvit existentiam*," before making the parallel statement, "*Essentia involvit conscientiam*." To be conscious of oneself is to be conscious of something indestructible, essence; for to grasp only that which tends to disappear (existence, for example) would be to make of consciousness "a tale told by an idiot."

In summary, consciousness of self is the most natural means by which man can understand himself as he is, i.e., as a form of being.

3. *Consciousness of self and the objective world*

May we not compare the outside world to a mirror? Man, seeing his reflection in it, ponders the question of his essence.

But the existentialists think that the reflecting surface precedes the being that has just looked into it. What matters to them is the life of the images in the mirror.

Their theory is false, though its opposite is difficult to demonstrate. In reality, without having a being, without being a being, man would not be conscious of himself or of his existence.

This reflection-existence, with everything that surrounds it—the objective world, the other, time, space, the body—must not be allowed to interfere with man's understanding of himself as an existence-being.

4. *Essence, consciousness of self, and Descartes' "Cogito"*

Human thought is conditioned by the consciousness of a thinking ego. What it seeks to grasp, even before its object, is the impetus of the action that calls it forth. The study of the mutual relationships between the subject and the object of thought is the basis of modern metaphysics; it has attracted such thinkers as Berdyaev and Nicolai Hartmann, whom we will meet further on. What must be mentioned here is that it is easier to demonstrate that consciousness of self precedes the *"Cogito"* than that essence precedes consciousness of self. For when it is a question of being, certainty arises on a level that goes beyond the rational.

To go beyond reason is not to destroy it by declaring it powerless. The processes of abstraction are not beyond the reach of a man who meditates; artists, philosophers, and ascetics can sometimes make use of them. However, trying to explain consciousness is an apparently contradictory task, for we can do so only by means of our consciousness itself.

Man gropes his way, then, across a dark road, trying to find the spiritual quintessence which constitutes his human nature, which is unattainable, for it is created in the image of God. His *cogito* cannot be conceived without consciousness of self; but that consciousness in turn requires an indefinable quantity summed up by essence, which cannot be explained in terms of reason.

5. *Consciousness of self-consciousness of existence, and the Other*

We are indebted to Gabriel Marcel for his deep insights into the correspondence between human consciousness and the Other. To him, "it is through others, and only through them, that we can understand ourselves." Against Cartesianism, he seeks to establish a metaphysics of "we are," in opposition to one of "I think." In the same way, he opposes Jean-Paul Sartre, who "...makes use of a Cartesianism which in other ways he has mutilated (since he has deprived it of the theology which crowns it) [and] is himself obliged to take the other only as a threat to my liberty; or, strictly speaking, as a possible source of seduction which it is very difficult not to interpret in a sadistic or masochistic sense."[1]

Marcel's criticism of these two *cogitos*, the theistic and the atheistic, seems quite cogent to us, but what can we say of a metaphysics that holds intersubjectivity to be the sine qua non of consciousness? The thesis appears to be profound and original, but it places too much emphasis on the human species at the expense of the human being. An individual cut off from the rest of humanity would remain superior to an animal. I am sure that a child raised by wolves would retain a minimal consciousness of self, however slight. And Adam, as the Scriptures describe him, perceives himself as a man prior to naming Eve *isha* (woman).

The human mind, the moral consciousness of each person, may likewise develop through contact with other people. But in as much as these two realities are basic to each individual, we cannot make them dependent on mutual influences, however imposing this interpretation may be.

We therefore consider it more appropriate to adopt the view that

---

[1] *The Mystery of Being*, Vol. 2: *Faith and Reality*. Chicago: Henry Regnery Company, 1970, p. 10.

human consciousness is the work of the Creator. In our view, each being exists independently of the billions of others, created one by one according to God's plan.

The Other also plays the mirroring role proper to the outside world; it invites consciousness to become aware of itself by showing it the image it reflects. But our thesis cannot avoid affirming that the consciousness of being precedes the consciousness of existence (hence of our encounter with the other): man *is* before he exists. It is the hand of God that keeps the revelatory flame of the consciousness of essence alive within us. This is what the human being and God the Creator have in common, despite the infinite distance that separates them.

The Essence-Being

Analysis of Essence

1. *Meaning of the word being*

The word "being" can be separated into two meanings. In addition to the gerund "being" (to be), there is a verbal adjective (or participle) "being."

Being-to-be corresponds to indagation, the search which is not embedded in time; but for the sake of convenience, we shall call it essence-being, that which "is" only in a restricted, never in an absolute sense (to accompany the unending rhythm of time). The essence-being, "which is immutable, passes through the life lived by the existence-being."

2. *Preliminary remarks: Essentia* and *existentia*

Man is a principle-being, but this being, *this* man, is necessarily existential. We said that consciousness of self—a divine reality, closely tied to essence—needed the world as a mirror. Likewise, essence needs to be embodied in the conscious human being, who might be called essence-existence-being.

11

The human paradox is to make essence and existence concomitant and inseparable. But in answer to the statement that man cannot be without existing, it must be emphasized that he would not exist without being.

Just as the faculty of vision, which is mental, does not come from the organ of sight, which is matter, the faculty of being, unlike that of existing, does not come from the world.

We recognize, of course, that if man "is" before he exists, he "is" only "in potentiality": since essence and existence are materially manifested in each person at the same time, the precedence of the former over the latter can be understood only as the precedence of the being in potentiality that tends to become existent.

Heidegger's system, for example, reduces human reality to what our existence will make it: man *is* his existence; he *is* what he makes himself. His "being in potentiality" is reduced to the role of an "abstract definition," in which man must not allow himself to be trapped. Thus, the notion of existence would be opposed not so much to "essence," but to "determinism" and "inertia." For his part, Sartre says: "Man is not what he is; he is what he is not." There is a certain lyricism in thus describing "the great adventure of being oneself." But it has been forgotten that man is *also* essence, and that despite the variations in the existential surface, the being that is within each person remains immutable.

Within each of us there burns a flame that may be compared to the igneous part of a volcano—the flame of pure being, which man may try to perfect (this striving for perfection is indeed man's work). But that flame, which gives man an idea of the Infinite, is impervious to external changes.

It is only as existence-being that man can undergo such changes, but the essence-being within him remains, by definition, immutable. But when eternity hovers too high above his understanding, he may succumb to the temptation to give in; he will then remain stuck in the role of an inferior being and will no longer consider himself as higher than existential beings. This is a defeatist attitude necessarily in contradiction with the destiny that man is intended to live out in the universe. His destiny is to be the world's consciousness—and to set himself apart, for example, from the swallow, which flies through vast spaces and looks at them, but does not know that it sees them.

Yet it is this type of outlook that atheistic materialism advocates in striving to show man without a soul and giving him a face reduced to the features of his existence. This is an attempt to escape the difficulty of the fact that man both *"is"* and exists; but the real solution is to recognize that essence precedes existence without separating man from his essence-being, for this would make the existential side of his nature lifeless as stone. If man is all of existence, existence is not all of man. By taking existence alone as an undeniable fact and repudiating essence, existentialism capitulates to the problem.

But the man it defines, a prisoner of existence, cannot help but rebel; it is the revolt "of the fist against the shackles," "of freedom against slavery." We say, rather, that it is the revolt of human intelligence, deprived of the only answer that could satisfy it. That answer is God.

And therefore, precisely because of this unmet need, man comes to glimpse the notion of creation; it can supply him with an explanation of his being. Is he not something created by the *ens increatum* (uncreated being)?

3. *Preliminary remarks: being as a being, world, thing, and spirit*

Jacques Maritain reminded us that Parmenides was the first in the history of Western philosophy to establish a doctrine of being. Before him, Heraclitus had formulated an essentially paradoxical theory: "That which is, is not, and that which is not, is, because everything is transformed and nothing remains, nothing remains of what is."[1]

Let us examine this sophism. The conclusion does seem to destroy the truth that serves as the premise. We might go so far as to say that since every human being changes, no one "is." As though change were a negation of the Being! To accept this theory would be to reduce the Being to dust, to strip it of all substance, to make of it a reality similar to time, which "is" only symbolically.

In fact, nothing, not even time, can change the essence of a being, which goes through all the ordeals of life without losing its nature. The permanence of being resists all change. Despite his transforma-

---

[1] Jacques Maritain, *Siete lecciones sobre el ser y los principios de la razón especulativa*. Buenos Aires: Ediciones Desclée de Brouwer, 1950, p. 88.

tions, man is certain of remaining identical to what he was and will be. And it is consciousness that shows him to be identical to himself, everywhere and at all times, in the past or in the future, and in all circumstances. The individuality of the being as a being is, in fact, the only certainty in the world. Though unintelligible and incomprehensible, it gives man a starting-point for the construction of his own ego.

For what is the material world? Man is unable to form an adequate idea of it. Human thought is limited to its superficial qualities, although a deeper inspection shows that it is made up of a few particles separated by vast spaces. Thus dissected, matter ultimately dissolves into nothingness, while man, on the other hand, can count on his being as an indestructible reality. This is because he is not limited to his physical person: he knows that he possesses the character of being owing to the unity of his mind and body. Objects represent nothing in themselves. Only human consciousness can attribute certain characteristics to material things; it is man who gives being to objects.

Take stone, for example. It acquires being only as a function of the person who sees it, understands it, and forms an image of it in his mind. Thus, matter is elevated to the condition of being only if it retains the indelible stamp of human influence. It has no meaning for other objects or for animals. Its meaning comes only from man.

Nor must it be forgotten that mind and matter are closely linked. It is difficult to dissociate the physical and the spiritual sides of human nature, in all its complexity.

Yet it is this unity which gives rise to the human being, in his mystery and perfection. The more perfect beings are, the more difficult it is to understand them. Nothing is more difficult for man than the search for his being, for it forces him to turn away from his existential pursuits and to go to the heart of the subject. Therefore, while man from the beginning of civilization has shown a taste for spiritual things, fear of the unknown, at least, has made him hesitate on the threshold of his being. Does he not, after all, prefer to launch himself into the distant spaces where he believes the infinite hides? In any case, he is as his Creator wished him to be, with his limitations as well as his freedom—that freedom which, of all human qualities, has made the greatest impression on philosophers throughout the ages.

4. *Aspects of essence*

a) Human joy and sorrow

Joy, as well as the other emotions, is a manifestation of man's essence. Laughter is a human phenomenon and is more than a mere mark of intelligence. An animal may appear intelligent, but is nevertheless barely capable of showing happiness, sorrow, annoyance, and surprise through its facial expressions. It is the soul which laughs, cries, saddens, becomes annoyed or surprised. But on the other hand, would a "pure spirit" be capable of laughter, since it could not materially manifest itself? And if it laughed, what would it laugh about? The world, man, or the megalomania of man setting himself up as God? In any event, laughter materializes on the human face; it is best expressed through human features.

The example of a house proves that joy is the privilege of man and not of material objects: when it is empty, we say that it is "sad," but let it be filled with its occupants, and life and joy return. It is through the human presence that a house partakes of human merriment. Why? Because an empty house is motionless, and to us, the "joy" of matter is its motion; thus, we feel no sadness at sea or in a forest. But this same "joy" without a human gaze upon it becomes mere turbulence, a movement toward a completely empty beyond. For all that is not the human soul, the future is nothing but a series of blindly destructive shocks. Beings journey toward death without becoming conscious of anything.

But in Heidegger's system, man himself escapes neither matter nor the world, and is reduced to a being "for death." Must he be compared to the walls of an abandoned house, doomed to collapse? Let us repeat what we said about the human dwelling: its stones are always the same, and it is the human presence alone that gives them a semblance of life. Human life, therefore, has a creative, hence imperishable quality, since it is capable of animating that which is inert.

However, while matter in itself has no meaning and is "nothing," it is not nothingness, either. Some try to reduce it to that concept, of which they are the authors. But if matter can reflect joy, for example, which is essentially human, it is because it can at least give support to the soul; it is merely incapable of feeling or living.

b) Essence and music

Music gives an idea of essence, for both are filled with life and at the same time empty of matter. They can reach their full magnitude without rubbing against the limitations of nature.

Music can touch our being and awaken the essence that slumbers in us. It fills us with a joy that is often tinged with sadness, and brings us to tears while at the same time making us smile. It also leads us to a conviction. Through music we know that human emotion at its peak exceeds common notions of joy and pain. It makes the pages of our lives turn more quickly, merging our past with our present.

Music rummages in our being, as it were, and strips the soul under the impact of love or despair. But this stripping seems to make it easier for the soul to take flight. Music has the unlimited strength necessary to make the transition from essence to existence.

But we cannot analyze the emotion of music by dissecting it. We must respect its secrets because it is life, and we would risk destroying it. To imprison it in words is impossible, for words are inert, while emotion is rich and active. It is a manifestation of the spirit, and may be compared to the surf of a vast ocean which touches other, infinitely distant shores.

c) Essence and saintliness

It is essence which illuminates the human past, and that is a proof of its predominance over existence. It is an immaterial force, and although nonhuman, is nevertheless within each person; not measurable, like a physical or mental force, but capable of increasing ad infinitum. That infinity, however, is attained only by the saints, who partake more of essence than of the human; for while they immmortalize being, it is at the expense of man as he exists in his imperfection.

The imperishable force of the Essence keeps alive forever in the minds of others the memory of exceptional beings. Thus, humanity in its entirety tends to "be" more. Saintliness bears within it the seeds of its survival.

d) Essence and the human gaze

If we observe the emotional process in the essence-being, we see that it springs from the depths of being, goes through human reality, and disappears into existence. Through that trinity—being/man/existence—it is, therefore, a process of materialization aimed at objective reality, although the spiritual "substratum" is preserved. The same mechanism is found in vision. Given the expressionless stare of the blind person, can we believe that the expression of the human gaze comes from the organ of sight? Is it not, rather, the result of the contact of a human essence with reality? The eyes, which in fact are nothing but matter—chromosomes, molecules, etc.—have a gaze which is much more than matter, which is existentialized essence, which is being living in man.

Vision, i.e., the act of seeing, is not only a physical act, a function of the organ of sight; it is a representation of what is seen. And what, then, is the expression of the human gaze? It is life, spirituality, reacting to that representation.

Thus the human role may be compared to that of a distillery; it distills the essence in matter because its position is both essential and existential.

e) Essence and the human face

The expression of the human face has no equivalent in the animal kingdom. If the eyes have been called the "windows of the soul," the entire face mirrors it as well. This explains why animal faces have no such expressiveness. We noted earlier that animals cannot laugh; since it is precisely essence that animals lack, we may conclude that the facial expression is a product of essence.

In poetic terms, we might say that the human facial expression is the hyphen between the spirituality of being and the existentiality of man, between essence and existence. It is in man that one ends and the other begins.

Furthermore, when we speak of nature's face, we are speaking of a world humanized by man's gaze. How beautiful nature is! It offers splendid landscapes—mountains, seas, sky; everything is beautiful, but beautiful to our eyes, which give life to that beauty. The motion taking place inside matter cannot be called "life" and is invisible to human eyes. Only painters can define nature, for they possess the essence and reveal it by painting. Thus absorbed in himself, the artist appears remote from everyone, as though out of this world.

But why does the face become expressionless when a person dies? Is it only life, then, which is expressed? Certainly not, for life, like expression, is a manifestation of the essence-being. Essence precedes both life and the expressiveness of the features.

The cause of attractiveness in a human face is man's ignorance about the secret of his being. The mystery lies in the entire face, not in its different parts. Through the mere motion of the features, without the aid of words, one can send a message more eloquent than spoken language; and that is what one relies on when the voice cannot be heard. It no doubt crosses the mysterious border between essence and matter.

f) Essence in man and in things: subject and object

The fundamental characteristic of essence is being-for-itself. Man is what he is without the help, in the final analysis, of his desires, his consciousness or even the world.

No doubt works of art, such as music, painting, or sculpture, also have a reflection of what we will call essence-being, that element which enables them to "be." But they "are" only because of the man who makes them.

Essence is the same in all these beings, and it is always just as inexplicable. The mystery surrounding it helps to characterize it, for the fact of being is not contingent.

Every being is predestined to come into the world and to create itself. Hence our theory of the being in potentiality, refusing to accept time as a thing in itself. But what then becomes of the power of time? How is it able to destroy the indestructible, the immortal? And if it is not capable of doing so, how could it prevent a being from creating itself?

Here it is necessary to recall N. Hartmann's doctrine concerning subject and knowledge, and also to criticize existential philosophy, which gives us an apparently distorted picture of a being which is not what it is. Hartmann declares[2] that the subject must go beyond itself. To know oneself, in fact, is to discover a transcendent truth; but this task seems impossible, since the subject is a consciousness, which makes the antinomy insoluble. We are faced with a dilemma: either consciousness is sealed, or it is capable of going outside itself, but it cannot be both simultaneously.

Essence differs from consciousness in that it is possessed by objects as well as by human beings, whereas consciousness is the exclusive

---

[2] Nicolai Hartmann, *Les principes d'une métaphysique de la connaissance*. Paris: Editions Aubier Montaigne, 1946.

privilege of man. Essence may even be understood independently of the "cogito."

Hartmann, however, seems not to distinguish between consciousness and subject, when he considers the subject in relation to the object of knowledge. Of course, the subject is consciousness, but it is not only that; it is also essence. And the ambiguity of consciousness disappears if being is defined as an elevation of essence to existence, for it is indeed being and not consciousness which goes through these three successive phases: consciousness, "cogito," and existence. It is by three degrees that the integral human being takes shape. It is a consciousness that in order to know itself seeks its essence.

Other beings are limited in their *ens* and are not capable of such an elevation, for they are dependent upon man. Nevertheless, essence persists in them; if they are not beings in themselves, they are at least objects. Their study leads us to sharpen the concepts of matter and energy, which are a challenge to human thought, for their basis eludes us. But the true solution is not to dematerialize them, as does contemporary physics, which no longer believes in essence!

A similar problem arises with respect to causality. We can state with N. Hartmann that reason does not explain reality in its duration. We try for a formulation of that permanence, but the formulas express only the relationship between permanence and change. All determinations of the being which is transformed are mysteriously, but necessarily, tied to substance.

The being does not change. What changes is the existing, which takes on multiple appearances. This leads to the problem of causality, for substance (structure possessing a content) is in itself of a causal nature; it is the chain that links each moment to the next. Because of it, the future has a kind of infinity; it is the shape of that which is preserved in time. Hartmann observes, however, that this "constant rustling" is basically irrational.

But with his reflections on substance, causality, and time, Hartmann is knocking on the secret door of reality. He has reached it by a roundabout route, the route of causality, which he views as the means by which the being can have access to the future without losing any of its substance. He certainly avoided the disintegration of being in time, but he seems to forget that the cohesive force which the human being possesses comes from his own essence. If it were otherwise, the notion of essence would be reduced to the Bergsonian duration, that unending time which enables the being to withstand destruction. It is essence alone, however, that guarantees the permanence of man's being.

We further note that Hartmann, in his analysis of being, defines essence as "pure being" or "pure subject." He adds: "Consciousness penetrates neither one nor the other. Of being, it apprehends only that which becomes object. Reason, which links subject to object in a relationship of knowledge, is only a narrow region squeezed between two forms of irrationality."

We recognize, of course, that consciousness cannot apprehend pure being (essence or essence-being), but a clear distinction must be made between pure being and subject. The subject owes its reality only to the existence of an object. The subject-object relationship is so close, although they are in opposition, that one cannot be imagined without the other. At best, being might be defined as the subject of objects, but it cannot be said that subject is essence. It is only one of the possible aspects of essence, once the being has attained consciousness and, through the practice of the *cogito*, is moving toward self-knowledge (hence knowledge of the world). But this process cannnot affect essence, which remains the *prima causa*, indestructible and perpetual.

We recognize that the subject-being is created when the principle-being becomes conscious of it, but we would modify Hartmann's formula. Rather than saying that "reason is squeezed between two forms of irrationality" (subject and object), we prefer to speak of two facts of a *spiritual* nature.

Whatever their relationship to human reason, subject and object are each other's reason to be. They are not equal, however; subject dominates, for it is one of the essential components of the integral man.

5. *A glance at several doctrines*

a) Hegelian being and essence—being or nothingness
We will examine and criticize the notion of being and of essence in Hegel, while acknowledging the greatness of his genius.

One of his theses is the following: "Being is related to essence as the immediate to the mediate." Sartre feels that this theory is based on the search for "the immediate in terms of the mediated, the abstract in terms of the concrete." He does not admit that this metaphysical process is the basis of being. For Sartre, "being does not hold the same relation to the phenomenon as the abstract holds to the concrete," nor as "one structure among others"; it is "the very condition of all structures and...the ground on which the characteristics of the phenomenon will manifest themselves."[3] Adopting Sartre's criticism up to a certain point, we ask how being can be separated from its essence, since it is essence that enables it to be. How can relationships like that of the mediate and the immediate be established between two things that are merely one? To separate being from essence would be tantamount to giving substance two roots, thus removing all unity from it, whereas being is one and indivisible. To accept such a separation would be to deny the substantiality which characterizes it, and to reduce it to mere matter made up of protons and electrons. But as we will see later, to accept the thesis of the divisibility of matter would be to destroy the substance of things.

Perhaps, after all, what Hegel calls being is merely the being that becomes man? In that case, one can indeed imagine a distinction between being, man, and existence-being, which make up the integral person.

Let us examine a second Hegelian thesis: "Things 'are,' in general, but their being consists of manifesting their essence." Sartre also questions this thesis: "It is not admissible that the being of things 'consists in manifesting their essence.' For then a being of that being would be necessary." The word "consist" is also difficult to accept, for how could we "determine a pure moment of Being where we could not find at least a trace of that original structure"?[4] Such a determination is the product of our understanding, which threatens to "fix" it.

"To affirm that being is only what it is," Sartre assures us, "would be at least to leave being intact so far as it *is* its own surpassing."[5] We

---

[3] Jean-Paul Sartre, *Being and Nothingness*. New York: Philosophical Library, 1956, p. 13.

[4] Sartre, *op. cit.*, p. 14.

[5] *Ibid.*

do not quarrel with his criticism, but we see in the "manifestation" of which Hegel speaks an extension of the being which appears in human guise; and in that case, it is necessary to assume an essence, for otherwise being would be merely empty, without consistency. In fact, it is being which enables man to manifest himself in the world.

Hegel also stated that "being passes into essence" and that "being presupposes essence." Everything depends on clarifying the meaning of the words "to pass" and "to presuppose." If "to pass" means "to change in manner," then the "passage" amounts to very little, for a thing cannot change while remaining the same. As for "presuppose," the word has such an abstract meaning that it does not "presuppose" a distinction between being and essence. The two formulas should, therefore, be modified and reduced to one: "Man presupposes the essence-being."

Hegel's fourth thesis is the following: "Although essence appears as mediate in comparison with being, essence is nevertheless the true origin." It is legitimate to define essence in relationship to being, since both partake of the same *ens*. But to make essence the origin of being is to refuse to make one equivalent to the other, for how could essence be its own origin?

Hegel further states: "Being returns to its foundation," and this statement seems to contradict the previous one, for how could being return to itself without having left itself?

In the final analysis, the explanation most useful in overcoming the difficulties of the Hegelian formulations is the following: "Pure being, from the standpoint of truth, takes the form of the immediate." We thus come back to the thesis which we analyzed first. However, if being, in order to become manifest, must go from the concrete to the abstract, how could it be the immediate in a pure state and have a relationship to the truth? It is necessary to distinguish between the existence-being, which needs matter in order to become manifest, and the essence-being which "is" immediately. Otherwise it is necessary to admit that the Pure Being is God, and to distinguish it from man, the mediator between the concrete and the abstract. But as we already stated, the being as essence has no need of the concrete. Let us recall that if man possesses the nature of an essence-being, it is because it was given to him by the Supreme Being which created him.

Thus, we reject the Hegelian definition of being as "the indetermination that precedes all determination," for if the Creator (whose image is man) were the indetermination, He would by that very fact lose the characteristics of unity and substance: does an indeterminate being have a reality? Can it logically represent the cause and the origin of the determinate? If we go back to the logical principle by which a cause cannot transmit to its effect that which it does not itself possess, we cannot accept that the indeterminate should create the determinate.

Therefore, to seek that which creates the determinate, we must take up the Hegelian problem of being and nothingness. For Hegel the absolute starting-point is an indeterminate. The problem of creation must be solved by opposing being to nothingness, as the determinate to the indeterminate: creation took place *ex nihilo*, being comes out of chaos, its origin was nothingness. We are led to believe in spontaneous generation, in which being issues forth without having been created.

But how could nothingness, as Hegel defines it—i.e., the indeterminate—be the origin of all determinations? We have already exposed this sophism as illogical and inconceivable.

To Hegel's definition of the nonbeing as "Pure Being," Sartre replies: "Is Nothingness not in fact simple identity with itself, complete emptiness, absence of determinations and of content?" Sartre closes his commentary on Hegel with this statement: "Pure being and pure nothingness are then the same thing. Or rather it is true to say that they are different; but, as here the difference is not yet a determined difference—for being and non-being constitute the immediate moment such as it is in them—this difference can not be named; it is only a pure opinion."[6]

Sartre is most certainly correct in chiding Hegel for having reduced being to "a signification of the existing." But by refusing to see that being is enfolded in essence, which is its foundation and origin, he finally comes to a Hegelian conclusion: being and nothingness are seen as two opposites, and the difference between them is a mere "opinion." Is this a reasonable doctrine? How can two opposing things be conceived of as a single reality? And how could being be nothingness? If nothingness "were," all the rest would be abolished.

6 Sartre, *op. cit.*, p. 13.

The pathetic tone of Hegel's formula ("There is nothing in heaven or on earth that does not contain in itself being and nothingness") should not make us forget that the master loves paradox, however dangerous it may be.

Other philosophers, desiring a balance, it seems, nevertheless accept nothingness as the counterpart of being. But nothingness, therefore, would be a boundary for being; and why should man paralyze his own abilities by drawing a circle beyond which he cannot go? That, however, is what these doctrines do. They reduce the integral being to the matter-being, and conceive of nothingness as a counterpart of being as a being.

Let us drop this thesis of a nonbeing capable of mounting an assault on being; ànd yet we come up against its perpetual "presence" in any analysis of being, which is all the more puzzling in that, according to Sartre, being does not need to go from the mediate to the immediate in order to affirm its presence; it is in itself affirmation, richness, positivity. Then why does being need nothingness? Whence the imperious necessity for the presence of nonbeing in the conceptualization of being?

There is something illogical in this coexistence of being and of nothingness; one might even say that to accept nothingness is to destroy the notion of being. There is nothing so futile as this effort to conceive of the existence of nothingness, since it is nonexistence in and of itself.

The only solution that can be offered as a substitute for Hegel's is to consider nothingness as a nonentity, and to conceive of creation as a being, the work of the Being, the Creator. Thus defined, not only can being dispense with nothingness, but nothingness becomes an evil which will attempt to swallow it up. But if man goes over to the side of evil, who will win this struggle? An uncertain battle, but above all, a futile one: it is sufficient to reject the concept of nothingness. Let us rid our minds of this idea of nonbeing, this mythological figure shaped by primitive imaginations. Let us give this evil no opportunity to spread, for though unreal, it might do great harm to being. The light being sheds is what the spirit needs in order to believe; it must flee the shadows of nothingness if it does not wish to succumb.

Those theories which appear to make nothingness the basis of being must be rejected. Being must have the way to freedom and eternity opened to it. Being cannot be nothingness; it can be only what it is, i.e., being.

b) Heidegger's critique of the "cogito"

In *Being and Time*, Heidegger criticizes the Cartesian *cogito*. This leads him to consider the basis of the statement "I am."

He, in turn, comes up against the mystery of being and of creation. Did God create the *ens creatum* (created being) by bringing it out of the shadows of nothingness, or did He prefer light—not the material light made up of protons and electrons, but the light which is never extinguished?

Baptized the "mystical prophet" by Nicolai Hartmann because he prefers statements to discussions, Heidegger expresses his deep conviction in the framework of his existential philosophy: the important question is the meaning of being, which Descartes seems to have considered useless, in view of the meaning he gives to his *cogito*: that of "being certain."

Heidegger reproaches Descartes chiefly for the ontological indeterminateness of the *res cogitans sive mens sive animus*. Descartes based his *Meditations* on medieval ontology, which still adhered to the definition of *ens* and *ens creatum*. He therefore gives a poor explanation of *sum*, despite the merit of his attempts to define *ego* and *cogitare*. As a matter of fact, Descartes' formula places *sum* and *cogito* on the same plane, which seems impossible to anyone who engages in an analysis of "I am."

Like Heidegger, we think that the statement "I am because I think" is tantamount to making both essence and existence dependent on thought, which is, however, only a manifestation of essence. On the other hand, we reject his way of opposing the *ens creatum* to the *ens increatum* in his analysis of Descartes." Moreover, our conception of being differs from his, which presents being as "flung into existence." His theory amounts to making essence a manifestation of existence, which we cannot accept.

Indeed, for us—contrary to both Descartes and Heidegger—essence is primary as a fundamental reality. It precedes consciousness of self and, *a fortiori*, thought, which is only the result of intelligence. Since consciousness is the object of analysis by thought, it stands to reason that it should precede thought.

Consciousness, being immaterial, can be detached from existence;

but it is through consciousness of self that man affirms himself, and does so as a unique being in face of the existential world; in the final analysis, consciousness has more contact with existence than with essence, for an infinite distance lies between essence and matter. We might even say that there could be no contact between them if man were not incarnate. Being, thanks to the human body which is made of matter, can touch objects; but it can also understand them because of intelligence. If man were merely essence, objects, space, and time— the necessary conditions of existence—would be useless; the Creator may have designed him that way, but the Fall flung him into the world. We will return later to the relationships between essence and existence, with man serving as a link between them; we will see that the formation of the human being amounts to a gigantic leap from the world of essences to the existential world.

c) Essence according to Spinoza

It is interesting to study Spinoza's original ideas concerning the essence of things and of man.

In his commentary, Léon Brunschvicg writes: "Abstract science draws from an individual's experience the conditions which make it possible to conceive of him, which constitute his essence."[7] The essence of man is therefore "a truth based on the total system of essences which constitutes the idea of God," and it remains the same both after and before the existence of things, Spinoza tells us.[8] This is made explicit by an example borrowed from mathematics: "Secants exist for the geometrician before they are drawn, as ideal essences, while some of them, in addition, have a physical existence."[9]

The central problem, therefore, being the relationships between essence and existence, it is interesting to examine this formula: "Essence gives meaning to existence; but only existence gives reality to essence; the thing having disappeared, essence disappears." We, of course, agree that essence gives meaning to existence, since it is the basis of it; likewise, we agree with the second statement, since only existence can make essence understandable and thus real to man. On the other hand, the last part of the formula cannot be applied to man.

---

[7] Léon Brunschvicg, *Spinoza et ses contemporains*. Paris: Presses Universitaires de France, 1951, p. 118.

[8] *Politics*, III, 1.

[9] Brunschvicg, *op. cit.*

We do not think that the death of the existing leads to the disappearance of its essence. It is quite possible that the image of an object, since it has no essence except that which it owes to man, should disappear with man's death; but the essence-being cannot die. It is indestructible by definition and by nature, since essence is based on the idea of God.

d) The essence of God according to Maritain

It is essential to recall the interpretation of the divine essence that Maritain presented in *Seven Lectures on Being*, in which he discusses the relationships between existence and knowledge: "Does God exist because He knows Himself, or does He know Himself because He exists?"[10] In other words, does essence arise from knowledge, or does knowledge arise from essence?

We may say that "God knows Himself because of His essence." But can we go further and postulate that He exists because He knows Himself, and that "His essence consists of knowing Himself"? Suppose that He does not know Himself—would He not exist? What is certain is that if He "were" not, He could not know Himself; therefore, His essence precedes His knowledge. It does not consist only of knowing itself, therefore, but of being all that it is—i.e., everything. Then why not consider it the fundamental basis of the infinite Being? Knowledge stems from existence, which, as we said already, comes after essence. Whether or not He knows Himself, the Infinite Being "is."

As for the human being, he exists only because he is a *particular* being, with all his individual and exclusive qualities. In man, the act of being what he is must be viewed as an absolute, because his essence was created in the image of his Creator. At the human level, consciousness plays the role that Maritain attributes to God's knowledge of God.

6. *Essence and man*

a) On man's essence

In contrast to existentialist philosophy, which seems to want to reduce man to existential materiality, we consider him above all as the essence of himself. Of course, as an existing being, man is matter

---

[10] Maritain, *op. cit.*, p. 181.

because of his body, but essentially, he is spirit, consciousness (we can point out in passing that psychoanalysis, the science of the unconscious, may be a science of nothingness: it does not attain the essence in what defines it). Likewise, the problems of the world, of space, of time, and so many others that trouble us, are nothing but existential, hence superficial phenomena.

However, knowledge of the "components" of being in its deepest sense is a real challenge to human intelligence. Contemporary philosophy struggles with it in vain, for it does not wish to go beyond considering man as an object flung into existence and into the world. The world and man are, to be sure, closely tied: the world is essential to man, and the world without a human gaze upon it would be a dead system. If the universe has a breath of life, it is due to the spiritual essence of its Creator, who holds all the atoms and particles in His control. Finally, man is closely tied to the world and to existence, but it is his essence which gives him his individuality.

b) Dialectic between essence and "decision"

The study of the being that becomes man places before us the problem of what Kierkegaard calls "decision."

The term is defined as "a positive manifestation of the will of man in despair." An element that precedes it, therefore, is despair. This, according to G. Marcel[11], occupies the central place in the philosophy of the father of existentialism (note that the fact of despair makes it necessary to pose the problem of a metaphysics: this is Kierkegaard's merit). However, if despair leads man to decision, it can no longer be said that decision defines him as an integral human being, for despair is of an existential nature.

We said that the essence-man was affirmation. Indeed, essence does not depend on human will. On the existential level, what opposes affirmation in man, who must struggle during his life, can only be *indecision*. But man, through the strength of his essence, can fulfill himself by surpassing existence and thus surpassing himself. His indecision may then be changed into Kierkegaardian "decision," but we consider it a manifestation of essence rather than a vital phenomenon of an existential nature.

c) Man reduced to his essence: is he merely dust?

---

[11] *Etre et Avoir*, Paris: Aubier, p. 150.

Any attempt to make man other than what he is, to elevate him to the infinite or to reduce him to nothingness, is foredoomed to failure. To try to reduce him to his essence would be to reduce him to dust. The most that could be accomplished would be to throw some dust on his corpse, for he will not be reduced to nothingness—a too convenient way to solve his problem, forgetting that he cannot be explained, and that, by definition, he does not understand himself. To conceive of him as a package of clay will never be sufficient!

On the other hand, man cannot be raised to the infinite, although his grandeur brings him close to it, because he does not consist solely of the infinite: he is "the synthesis of the finite and the infinite," of matter and spirit, of small and large, of being and existence. Man's complexity is a mixture of nothingness and of the infinite, which, by combining in this way, lose each one of their own characteristics in order to form this organized disorder. Man is made up of everything: of all values and of their opposites.

Freud seems to have tried to limit man to his sexual problems. Heidegger seems to have seen nothing in him but his existence. We, however, think that man can be reduced to nothing except man. Human vision is too small to encompass the entire human portrait, even the artist cannot help fragmenting it in portraying it. We may therefore compare man to a marble colossus, which consists not only of a statue but also of a pedestal. This pedestal is being. As for the sculpted figure, it is not pure marble, and also contains mud; but the whole structure rises to an almost infinite height.

There is something of the infinite, too, in man's anxiety to fulfill himself as an integral human being, even if the human essence, which is one of his components, gives him a power similar to that of the Creator. What gives man anxiety is the fact of being the sum of everything, from matter to spirit: an indivisible whole.

Therefore, we do not wish to reduce man to his essence. Even though we do not believe that he could be "reduced to dust" in this way, we know that an infinity of things in him, which are also him, would be annihilated.

7. Being—Essence—Foundation

a) Complexity of essence

The essence-being is something whole, complete, something that "is" by itself, without the need of existence. Existence, on the other hand, is essential to man; the two possible degrees of being—essence-being and existence-being—are concentrated within him. He makes a whole, complex, and perfect system, which constitutes the integral human being.

Although death can rob man of existence, being can never be taken from him.

b) The depths from which being emerged

Being emerged from a kind of abyss: its nature is profound, incomprehensible, dizzying. But although we do not know what that abyss is, it does not represent nothingness, but the medium in which being was created, shaped by divine hands. We might say that the influence of that medium has left something shadowy in the human being. As though drawn to the mystery of the chasm in which he was created, a man who gives himself up to his thoughts is said to be "lost" in them. Unable to describe these depths clearly enough, some have called them "nothingness" but, as we said, it is unthinkable that being should come out of nothingness; being is not nothingness.

However, man's inner nature has acquired in our minds the characteristics of that abyss from which he emerged. He has its depth, its incomprehensibility, its mystery, its shadow. And in order to define the endless process by which beings, one by one, emerge into the foreground of being, we can do no better than to fall back on the Portuguese expression *moto-continuo*. Giving up, then, on a satisfactory explanation of the resulting product, the signs of which are nonetheless visible to us, how could we dare try to imagine the original process of the creation of being? Creation is a secret, an enigma, the solution of which hides in the unknown regions of being, those which take up no space and are unaware of time.

Creation emerged from the depths of chaos. Darkness, the Bible tells us, became light—a metaphor signaling the emergence of being, for being, like light, is a gift of God.

Emerging at the surface of the world and of existence, man has a tendency to forget those depths; he has known them, however, for he is spirit. But now only this world meets his gaze, which is human, for it is as an existing being that he lives in the world.

For one who wishes to escape the world, there is no solution but to seek his essence. Consciousness of self lights a little of the way for him between existence and essence, but it is only a pale reflection of the light of being; it was contaminated by contact with the outside world. True light is not that which illumines, but that which creates.

c) Analysis of the "essence" of being

Essence is incomprehensible to man. It is to essence that we should apply the expression "a gap between my being and my self," which G. Marcel used to define existence, viewed as a "previous state" (I am before I live).[12] For us, on the other hand, it is essence which is that "previous state." The existence-being partakes of the objective world, while essence divides from matter. The best comparison we can find to help define it is still that of "light": essence is the hyphen between man and God.

Its universe, therefore, is a limitless world which space and time can neither define nor fill, and where existence is "seized with vertigo," to use the Platonic phrase. If man tries to penetrate it, however, from the platform of his existence, he falls into the depths; he risks destroying his intelligence. Thus man must be resigned to never knowing himself completely. He may transform matter and the world, but he will never know essence, because it is pure creation, lying beyond (existential) space and time. The relationships between essence and existence are contingent: man wavers between existence (imagining that he is born to die) and essence (which destines him for immortality). But as essence is incomprehensible to him, he is tempted to ignore it.

In ignoring it, however, in leaving it beyond his grasp, he enables it to remain intact and to preserve its purity. Eggenspieler does in fact speak of a "cry" of being, which reaches man's ears and would be the voice of consciousness. But it is only a distant echo, the sound made by a much deeper voice, itself imperceptible to that which is existent, for it belongs to the world of being. Moreover, some thinkers, such as Heidegger, refuse to recognize that voice. Not believing in being, they are forced to think that consciousness is the voice of nothingness. What is nothingness, if it can be heard?

---

[12] *Positions et Approches*, Paris: Aubier, p. 25.

The struggle that man wages to get a real idea of himself is comparable to his struggle for daily bread. The world will not provide him with what his being needs to live; he must first ask for it by kneeling before the Creator, then by getting up to begin his search. What does it matter if the quest does not succeed? To undertake it is already a solution. For it liberates man, the prisoner of the world.

Of the Abstract and the Concrete

1. *Being and the transition from the abstract to the concrete*

We have stated our position, warning of the danger involved in accepting nothingness into thought. We will now further explore the Hegelian problem of the transition from the abstract to the concrete, which is a transition from the immediate to the mediate, since it begins with the object (immediate, because it exists by itself) used as an intermediary by the ego in order to gain consciousness of itself.

This question, when approached from a different angle, shows us that the conscious being also exists by itself as a function of its essence. It is thus necessary to clearly distinguish these two processes. One consists in becoming conscious of an object through perception of its image; the other consists in becoming conscious of oneself, which is immediate because it is "by itself." Imagine, for example, that Robinson Crusoe had been alone on his island since early childhood. He would first become conscious of himself, and only then would he seek to know the space around him. But the process would be so rapid that he would not know what he had become

33

conscious of first. The Creator would have provided him with every-thing necessary for existence (which does not mean essential for consciousness of self). Thus, the multitude of material objects is perceived by man, but the idea he forms of himself does not depend on his perception. For that matter, if space is necessary to man so that he may live, is it necessary for the practice of conscious thought? And does a being need it after death?

No, the primary phenomenon of consciousness of self is undoubt-edly independent of matter. But could man then also abstract himself from matter? Could he separate the abstract from the concrete in himself? Ecstasy may be considered a proof of this possibility. How-ever, man is so deeply embedded in existence, plunged by his work into the core of matter, and surrounded by so many material objects, that he ultimately convinces himself that it is through these objects that he becomes conscious of his being.

Consciousness of self may take two forms, depending on whether it is connected to existence or to essence. As existence, it is filtered through the medium of the concrete, while as essence, it takes place immediately, disregarding matter. In the "atmosphere" of essence, everything that is matter dissolves; the essence-being separates from earthly clay, so as not to contaminate its proper realm (the Scriptures state that "at the end of centuries" God will destroy what remains of matter, so that being may be revealed in all it fullness). Thus, man must prevent his being from falling back to the level of his material body, although it is sufficient to itself; we reject, therefore, both the Hegelian conception which threatens to reduce it to a lesser being (considering it a mere by-product of the transition from the concrete to the abstract) and the Sartrian explanation, which threatens to reduce it to nothingness.

To affirm the full reality of our being is tantamount to celebrating its victory over both the corporeal world and nothingness.

It is important, however, to elevate the concept of being above its struggle with nonbeing. For in fact, we know as little of this battle as we know, from the story of the Apocalypse, about the confrontation between God and the rebel Angel. If, however, we also believe that man can abstract himself from matter, we should rather glorify in him that which constitutes his essence-being and does not need the body in order to obtain light.

2. *From the concrete to the abstract*

Does one go from the concrete to the abstract or from the abstract to the concrete? That is the alternative posed by Hegel and Sartre. But a thinker like G. Marcel, basing himself on reality, manages to escape the dilemma.

For it is consciousness of self, as a reality *in itself*, that enables man to conceive of the abstract, as well as to touch the concrete. By itself it can attain the two realities, the objective and the subjective. But it can attain them only because consciousness gives them a meaning. An incomplete meaning, for the objective world, like the subjective universe, keep their secret hidden in the complexity of their structures. This secret is their essence, which is as incomprehensible as that of man.

What, for example, is the notion of light? What is the concrete? The abstract? Were they made for being, or was being made for them?

One no longer needs to ask these questions if one admits that there is a God who is the Creator. Everything in creation has its reason to be (*raison d'être*). Light is made for the universe; thus, the concrete and the abstract are seen as two mental worlds which come into contact through the presence of a conscious being. Each of these two worlds can be explained in terms of the other when consciousness acts as their intermediary. Their relationship is that of the objective to the subjective; and it is man's conscious intelligence which, according to God's plan, marks the final boundaries of their two domains.

3. *Concrete and abstract in the analysis of essence*

Can we speak of abstract and concrete in regard to essence? It is neither concrete nor abstract. It is not concrete, in the sense that it does not belong to the reality of the world, except when it takes the shape of a human being. As for the process of abstraction (beginning with the concrete), it cannot lead to essence either, for it is real in its own way, and cannot be merely the result of an abstraction.

Essence, in fact, is a "something" that wavers between the concrete and the abstract, thus establishing a certain relationship between them. While neither one nor the other can encompass it, both nevertheless tend to destroy it. Thus, the rationalists try to convert it into image and the existentialists into inert matter. But essence is neither concept nor substance, neither unreal nor existential; it is pure spirituality. This pure spirit can take a human body, but it is independent of existence and can therefore continue to "be" after death, in eternal life, because essence is the very principle of life.

How can we then deny that essence precedes existence?

Being, Act, and Potency

1. The potency of being and the corporeal world

In the presence of living beings and corporeal things, each subject to its own rhythm, one has the intuition of a continuous unfolding of being. This cannot be reduced to the blind transformism of the materialists, not to Heraclitus's formula, "Everything changes"; it even goes beyond the Bergsonian "vital force" or Heidegger's "race toward death." It corresponds rather to "something that would be in potentiality" and "would become ever more," that is, to the very essence of things (and of man) as "matter-beings." This process of becoming is indeed, in Aristotle's classic definition, "going from potency to the act," by which matter "receives a form."

The existence of the world impinges on our consciousness and leads us to think that it has always been in potentiality. Before it existed, was it not in a latent stage of creation?

Take the example of a bud before the final flowering. It is a flower in potentiality, i.e., it contains within itself all the energy necessary to make it bloom; thus, the world, conceived as what it ought to be, was already the world before taking the shape that makes it visible to us. Its appearance at each moment is only the final detail of divine creation. Everything in the world is thus a thing "in potentiality" and can take one or another shape depending on God's plan. Since God is the Creator, His plan can only be creation; it would be a contradiction in terms had he not given being to that which eternally resides within him.

2. *The being in potentiality as a logical reality*

This thesis of the preexistence of being, linked to the infinity of the Creator, may be suspected of pantheism. It is important, therefore, to define it and to underscore its limits. The "being in potentiality" does not precede creation (like the Creator Himself), neither in its essence form nor in its existence form. However, its creation appears as a necessity.

This thesis leads us to postulate the reality of the being in potentiality as the outcome of a logical, highly rational process which therefore possesses something divine.

Being, prior to existence, is a possibility which has a very high probability of realization. It is something undefinable, but it is already *something*.

In the search for the origins of being, our argument takes the form of a logical proof, in which our *mens* goes ahead of the Creator (the possessor of both the seeking *mens* and of the being that is sought). A kind of vertigo, to use Plato's expression, can therefore prevent the mind from grasping the rest of this argument.

Logic, of course, is not always safe. Sometimes it locks us into a circle that limits our perception. But if it is well developed and based on solid principles, it leads to unassailable conclusions. For that matter, are the data furnished by experience always accurate? If Newton, as the story goes, discovered the laws of gravity through a falling apple, did not Einstein come closer to the truth than he did? Yet he did not rely on experimental data; his system is built on logic.

Thus, in our analysis, it is necessary to escape from time and space in order to get a perspective and disregard the external framework. Despite the paradox, it is necessary to distance ourselves from the man-being we are in order to know him better; and if it is true that we live in a cave, we should at least place ourselves on a height in order to observe ourselves. Being needs to be viewed from above. Even as a being in potentiality, it must be referenced to the Creator, for it is only from the standpoint of its creation that its potentiality as a being can be understood.

God, therefore, gives us the light that illumines these darknesses, in the aura of which nothingness is no more than a speck of dust. Yes, indeed, when being reveals itself, to what is nonbeing reduced?

3. *The being in potentiality and the being for death*

In a paradoxical way, being "is" even before "being." Indeed, it "is" in potentiality even before it exists in the world. The same logic might be used to show that the human being is a dead being before death, because he moves inexorably toward death.

There is a difference, however: being is creation, affirmation, while death is negation, destruction. Yet if one can understand that something may be latent in that which is affirmative and creative, one cannot accept it as a negative fact, a nonentity. To try to equate the being in potentiality prior to life with the being in potentiality before death is as unjustifiable as to infer the reality of nothingness as a consequence of being, as Sartre seems to propose doing.

But if one rejects such an equation, it implies the persistence of being after death, and this, therefore, confirms the thesis of the being in potentiality: if death does not destroy being, but only man, we conclude that being does not die and that it continues to be in forms different from the human reality. Death cannot destroy being, since being-as-a-being is a reality and cannot possibly coexist with death. If death could destroy it, it would be revealed as stronger even than the principle which permitted the creation of that being. But that principle cannot stem from a negative factor.

Thus, there is nothing left for us but to bury the specter of Death.

Concerning Anxiety

1. The anxieties of a being are the anxieties of being

The anxieties of the conscious being stem from the very fact of being. In exchange for his privileges, by the very fact that he is conscious, the being bears a heavy burden of anxieties; he must shoulder them in his ascent, which is by definition impossible, as with the rock of Sisyphus, for arrival at the top means death, that is, loss of that same consciousness of self which is characteristic of the human being.

It is because of his essence that man is subject to torment and despair. It should be clear, however, that it is man who despairs, and not the being, which is higher than man. Nonetheless, the importance Kierkegaard gives to despair is justified; this sentiment corresponds to the anxiety man feels because he exercises his capacity for being in the world. Despair cannot be imagined on the level of plant life. Only man can feel it, for his conscious life is capable of a synthesis of happiness and unhappiness.

For man, the fact of being is already an enigma; the search for its solution brings him both pleasure and pain.

These, therefore, are the elements that make up his life: pleasure and pain, happiness and despair. As an essence-being, he partakes, after all, of the objective world. His anxiety is related to the destiny of matter, which travels through time and space toward nothingness. For matter is not a thing in itself. It has been shown to be destroyed by motion, and is there anything that does not move? Man on earth, the earth around the sun, the sun and the entire universe in a flight toward the infinite. Man is caught in this whirlwind, but differs from it precisely by his capacity for anxiety. If the universe runs blindly, if energy tends to return to nothingness, if man—as matter—panics while following the same route, he is the only being to suffer from it, for he is lucid; he sees, understands, and experiences his own destruction.

One possible reaction, as man contemplates his existence and his essence, is to see only nothingness and not a solution to the enigma of creation. That is the source of despair, but if man despairs, it is because he is matter; matter encloses him and limits his freedom. To be sure, it is Being that emerged in the world, clothed in a human shape, but Being poured into matter; it must free itself through self-affirmation as a spiritual being. Within that matter, however, man is exposed to doubting everything—himself, the spirit, and even the Creator.

It is more because of his material condition, therefore, than his situation in time and space, that the being is tempted to despair. If he were not destined to follow the laws of existence, and particularly the law of death, man would know nothing of such a temptation. Therefore, it may be said that human anxieties stem from man's "Fall," which tied his being to matter in existence. Anxiety, a product of man's existential life, appears in this perspective as the punishment for a crime that must be expiated. It is, therefore, after all, a spiritual phenomenon, spontaneous in man who is dissatisfied with his condition. And the more man perfects himself, the more he feels anxiety in all its magnitude: he despairs because he *exists*, and also because he is conscious that he "is."

Despair, therefore, is both something material that must disappear along with life, and a sign that goes beyond this contingent life. For man, of course, trembles at the thought of death, but his fear is mainly that of the unknown; we know that doubt is even crueler than the certainty of extinction. Nothingness is not unknowable, and if man were destined to be transformed into nothingness, he would hardly need to be afraid. But if, after death, he encounters the All, he will fear what he is to find, not knowing the nature of that All.

Thus the anguish is great, for it is the search for something lost, which cannot be found within the bounds of space and time; the Being "lives," as it were, outside this world. Despair issues from the principle rather than the end result, from creation rather than death; it is the characteristic of the spirit which is impotent in the face of such secrets.

2. *Metaphysical anguish*

Alfred Eggenspieler[1] captures metaphysical anguish precisely: "In settling into essence, we heard the piercing cry of existence. The instant finally triumphed over any ideal elevation into duration. Was it not the instant that suggested to us the first surprise of being?" He also evokes "the metaphysical anguish in the depths of understanding" in Bergson and the Augustinian uneasiness of "*quando consolidabor in Te.*"

This anguish is deeper than Kierkegaardian uneasiness, because it cannot be reduced to the psychological reaction of man at large in the world and totally ignorant of his whereabouts in time and space. It is spiritual by nature: it is man's recognition of his conditions of existence, which make his being a prisoner of matter. Anguish thus raises man to his essence.

Man, to be sure, is blind and deaf, but his consciousness is a sort of opening toward being, revealing to him the presence of an enigma. Human understanding, however, is unable to resolve it clearly; it is subject of doubt, to vertigo, as Plato says. One might also say that essence is like a glaring light which blinds.

3. *The error of Søren Kierkegaard*

Kierkegaard's error consists, perhaps, in viewing anxiety too much as a reflection of human contingency, whereas to us it seems to have

---

[1] Alfred Eggenspieler, *Durée et instant.* Paris: J. Vrin, 1933, p. 143.

deeper roots. To us, anxiety is the cry of being, lost in the world and far from the God who created it.

Man suffers from seeing the futility of his efforts to know himself; his physical eyes barely serve to penetrate matter. But to make anxiety a purely human phenomenon would be to "transport the ocean to a hole dug on solid ground, among the sands of the shores." For its origin is not uniquely existential. Far from being created in this world, it is rooted in the fathomless recesses of Being, and if one denies that, one plunges man even more solidly into the mire of matter. Would that not make his despair still worse?

In reality, anxiety is like the cry of a soul flying toward God. Let us recall the words of St. Augustine: "*Quando consolidabor in Te!*" They show that anguish may very logically lead to prayer: it contains the demand that God show us what being is.

4. *Cosmic anguish*

If man manages to escape from Mother Earth, this world would lose its purpose, which is to be the existential environment created for man. But if that escape occurs, which would lose more as a result, man or his planet? On a different planet, man would be faced with the following alternative: either become master of a new world or be destroyed by it.

But if man does not find the expected new world, if his mad haste to escape from the earth has brought him to regions inhabited by nothingness, how will he bring life to dead places? And realizing that the kind of infiniteness which attracted him is not the Infinite, how will he be satisfied with it? The farther he goes into lifeless space, the farther he will go from his essence and the more lost he will feel in that endless, meaningless void.

What can his reaction be then, except despair and a mortal anguish born of his own alienation? At a time when man should seek to understand himself, in offer to rescue what little remains of the human and the spiritual from atheistic materialism, his exclusive concentration on outer space is somewhat aberrant. One is simply trying to escape from oneself when one turns to that empty expanse which is like "a piece broken off from the Infinite." The lure of space is like that of the bottomless depths, and in the final analysis, it resembles the lure of despair: human anguish can only worsen if it becomes cosmic, confronting a new unknown where man will feel more lost than ever. The farthest he goes from himself, the more lonely the traveler feels.

Ontological Determinism

1. *Being and death*

"All men are mortal." Indeed! The being within each person is not on the road to death, but to that eternal life which Bergson called "God's abode." For being, because it is affirmation and abundance, is filled with "life."

Submerged in existence, man sometimes refuses to raise his sights higher than the most obvious reality, that of material life. Disdaining to believe in an afterlife (or perhaps fearing a cold reception there), he prefers to believe in death, and invites his fellows to participate in its universal concert.

How to describe this concert of death? Let us say that the sonata of Nothingness is played there. Obeying its rhythm, despiritualized man is already a corpse before burial. It is logical that he should have that corpselike appearance, since he has lost his resemblance to the God of life: making a veritable cult of death, he allows nonbeing to dwell in his own house.

Our era offers an astonishing contrast between man in a materialist civilization, where he shatters the atom but disintegrates himself, and man who is a being on the road to life. At bottom, however, the paradox is clear: man constructs himself by annihilating himself; the more he despairs, the more he asserts himself; the more he suffers, the more he lives.

However, in order to crystallize him and make him human, his essence, which is eternal in him, gives him his second wind in his climb. If the corrosive effect of nothingness could not destroy being, why despair?

2. Man is a "being of distant places"

In his critique of Heidegger's phenomenology of nothingness, Sartre says that even for the *Dasein* there is a constant possibility of coming face to face with Nothingness and of discovering it as a phenomenon: this explains anguish. It is said to be like a state of drunkenness, during which man comes in contact with nothingness, forgetting his own reality. But in such a state of semi-prostration, how could man find the truth? The nothingness he confronts is only the shadow of reality, and man in the grip of this anguish runs the risk of mistaking a ghost for something real.

This anguish can arise only from a double negation. On the one hand, human reality looms as an emergence of being from nonbeing; on the other hand, the world is "suspended" in nothingness. But is not reality the fact that being organized itself as the world, beyond the world itself?

In any case, human reality as Heidegger defines it—a "being-in-the-world"—can give the being organized as the world the appearance of a totality only by surpassing it, by means of a certain retreat. Such a surpassing is the very precondition for the resurgence of the world as such, carried out by the *Dasein*, which is a for-itself. Thus, it is by surpassing the world that the *Dasein* would itself appear as "not being in itself and not being the world."

Sartre asks in reply: "If I emerge in nothingness beyond the world, how can this extra-mundane nothingness furnish a foundation for those little pools of non-being which we encounter each instant in the depth of being?"[1] And he concludes: "Nothingness can be nihilated

---

[1] Sartre, *op. cit.*, p. 19.

only on the foundation of being; if nothingness can be given, it...lies coiled in the heart of being—like a worm."[2]

Conversely, it is only in nothingness that being can be surpassed. And it is after it is surpassed that the *Dasein* brings about the contingency of the world. The question that arises is the following: "How does it happen that there should be something instead of nothing?"

In any case, man remains separated from what he is by the entire breadth of the being he is not. He reveals himself to himself from the other side of the world, and comes back to internalize himself at the horizon: man is a *being of distant places*.

We adopt this expression of Heidegger's because existence and pre-existence are one and the same in the human being. Unlike the German master, however, we cannot accept that human reality should appear only because it is "invested in the world." Why not rather accept the precedence of reality over the world, owing to its essence? Why not stick with the notion of being predestined to be? This idea is not incompatible with that of "being from distant places"; let us conclude by saying so.

3. *Ontological determinism*

The determinism that some writers find in the evolution of life (be it historical, physical, or biological) seems for others to be nothing more than a theoretical possibility. Is not history filled with surprises that throw it off course? Likewise, in physics—according to Planck's quanta theory—are not certain explosions, which imply a loss or an increase of mass or energy, completely unforeseen by our calculations?

If determinism were a reality, it should enable man to see how his life will turn out, and humanity would be master of its history, as of the world. At any rate, it would be the doing of man rather than of things.

In a sense, traces of it can be found, for the human being, in the development of his personality, the seed of which lies in his essence. A person may be born with a gift for music, science, or politics, and his

---

[2] Sartre, *op. cit.*, p. 21.

entire being will tend toward one of these activities, revealing him as an artist, a scientist, or a statesman.

Man at birth already is what he will become. In other words, he "is" before he exists. He is an integral being, which possesses in potentiality, as though on the sly, all that he will later become.

Determinism, therefore, must be an internal force rather than an external compulsion. Man can create himself through abilities that are latent in him. He cannot escape from himself, were it to create a new world, without the risk of destroying himself. And this implies consciousness of self; without it, determinism is only a blind force. Man keeps the direction of his activity in a line that is his own from birth to death.

But is there a connection between death and each destiny? What is the cause of death? Does it stem from the laws of the outside world, or is it inscribed in the individual history of each human being?

It may be defined as the exhaustion of the life forces; consequently it assumes a kind of predestination for each being. A person whose own thinking and will have defined the meaning of his life more or less chooses his death. Both are stages in the development of his being, according to laws established by the very essence of the integral human being. Man cannot escape the limitations of his own forces, but they leave him a vast enough field in which to live out what he is. His life, too, might be compared to "a piece torn from the infinite," because God, even while placing him in time, wished to create him in His image.

4. *What will I be tomorrow?*

The Greek thinkers taught man to wonder about himself. But what answer has he found? May human intelligence—which is nevertheless said to be evolving—be helpless in face of the problem of being?

Heidegger tried to advance the solution of this problem by postulating that the being is an *ens*, of course, but one which in addition has a meaning. For his part, G. Marcel sees in the being that which withstands an analysis that reduces the facts of existence to elements increasingly devoid of intrinsic or meaningful value. He writes: "Is there such a thing as being? What is it? Yet immmediately an abyss opens under my feet: I who ask these questions about being, how can I be sure that I exist?"[3]

Descartes found that asssurance in consciousness of self. But where does consciousness itself come from? Does it come from nothingness—as Heidegger suggests—or from another being, higher than man? One question leads to another, and good minds realize that they are unable to answer questions such as "What is being?" or "What am I?"

Let us try to ask a slightly different question by changing the verb tense and asking, "What will I be tomorrow?"

Other factors then intervene, such as time, the contingent, the unpredictable. If being resists itself, will it withstand the fall into the chasm of the future? Faced with the drama of his existence, faced with the mystery of life, man can refuse to answer the question, "What will I be tomorrow?" But his refusal would be akin to despair.

On the other hand, if man has faith in himself, if he does not consider time as an element foreign or hostile to himself, then in spite of his limitations, he can look his future in the face.

While it is true that contingency depends on space and time, as well as on our position between those two infinites, it also depends on us, who imagine it. Man must therefore confront the contingency arising from his presence in the world, and, strengthened by his struggle against it, must recognize that those two "infinites" were conceived by his own intelligence. Space, of course, exists as a function of matter; but matter exists as a function of man, who is essentially spirit. As for time, far from appearing as an infinity it corresponds to an "emotion-time," linked to the life of the person who is conscious of it.

Thus shown to be facing two pseudo-infinites, man is able to understand that he is the only being capable of withstanding the power of the spirit-man which stems from the divine infinity. Once the statement has been made, "The future is man," the question "What shall I be tomorrow?" comes down to the answer "Become what you are." For man will never succeed in dominating his being.

---

[3] Gabriel Marcel, *Philosophy of Existence*. Philosophical Library, Inc., 1959, p. 6.

Being and the Infinite

1. *The human infinite*

Each man is a special stage on which the human drama is played. In each person there is a titan chained by his Creator: he possesses the infinite within himself, but cannot free himself from matter. In each person there is an Icarus with wings too fragile; the only flight to which he can aspire is toward his internal self, in the opposite direction from interstellar space. But this internal world is like an infinite reduced to a speck: if we intuitively feel the infinite bubbling within our being, in reality our physical self is an infinitely small image of the Infinite that is God.

This smallness of man is nonetheless a magnitude that cannot be humanly measured. And it would probably be more accurate to abandon comparisons of a geometric nature and to speak of forces, of energies, or potentialities, ever ready to burst forth.

2. *The "infinitization" of the self in Kierkegaard*

In addressing the problem of essence and of existence, Kierkegaard sensed the drama of the human being, torn between spirit and matter.

He explained it as follows: "The self is the conscious synthesis of infinite and finite which relates to itself and whose goal is to become itself, which can only be by relating to God. But to become oneself is to become concrete, which cannot be done in the finite or in the infinite, since the concrete which one becomes is a synthesis. Evolution consists, therefore, of moving indefinitely away from oneself in an 'infinitization' of the self, and of indefinitely returning to oneself in a 'finitizing.' However, the self that does not become itself remains desperate, whether it knows this or not. Yet at each instant of its existence, the self is in a process of becoming, for the potential self does not really exist, and is only what is to be. Thus, so long as it does not succeed in becoming itself, the self is not itself; but not to be oneself, that is despair."[1]

This extraordinary paragraph from the Danish master is much more deserving of repetition than of comment. The only way to make it even more impressive is to compare it with the myth of Prometheus Bound. The despair into which man plunges when his drive toward himself is broken—is that not the same as the stormy revolt of the Titan? And is not "infinitization" symbolized by the volcanic fire which the hero tried to steal in order to reach heaven?

Another mythical figure appears in this backdrop—Sisyphus. For our life—shunted between "finitization" and its opposite—resembles the rock that goes up almost as high as the heavens, and then falls back again with all its weight.

---

[1] Søren Kierkegaard, *Traité du Désespoir*. Paris: Gallimard, 1949, pp. 89-90.

Various Thoughts

1. Man, the first enigma in the universe

How can we explain the fact that among the great mysteries, like those of the universe, the creation, or death, man stands out as the primary one? Because man, as an essence-being, transcends the universe. His internal world is an infinite that even he cannot understand. Thanks to science, man is learning more and more of the world's secrets, up to several billion light years. The universe, it is predicted, can be measured, for it is finite. But not man!

The cosmos long appeared to be unlimited, simply because we could not imagine its boundaries. Nevertheless, they exist, but only the wisdom of the Creator knows them. Unable to imagine them, man concluded that they did not exist. In any event, they will be revealed to us at the end of time, when the world again becomes nothingness.

For his part, the human being has infinite proportions, for he is created in the image of the Infinite Being. But then might we speak of an equality between those two infinites? Was this not the way that man rebelled against his creator, which is why the Scriptures say that God repented of having created him? In reality, the perfect God cannot regret his work, which is perfectly worthy of his love, both the cosmos and man. But he created man in order to be loved by him, and one does not wait for love without impatience.

Yet each person's history is made up of emotions felt in the present and cut from the plane of universal love, emotions that vanished into the past. Their importance is infinite, because man is essence: that is the reason why he is an enigma.

Man is emotion, as matter is energy. He can be neither the present, the past, nor the future completely; all three are concentrated within him. He is, in some fashion, a synthesis of what he has experienced and is about to experience, as Bergson showed. Furthermore, while he considers the objective world, man will never grasp it *in toto*, because he himself is part of it and thus lacks perspective. Only his death enables him to situate himself outside the cosmos.

It is by turning to his inner world that man can find happiness, for then he can understand the smallness of the seemingly unlimited universe, as well as the infinite grandeur of his being, the image of the divine Infinite. The closer he feels to the Creator, the more he experiences his freedom to love and to be.

2. *"Nosedive" toward the Being*

The thinker who, upon analysis, changes his plan and goes from the objective world to the world of essence is like a pilot who stops allowing himself to be airborne and goes into a "nosedive."

The routine emotions of existential life held him in suspense, as it were, within a limited and ultimately inconsistent space, but a space familiar to his mental life. To him, becoming conscious is like a spiraling plunge. And there he is, faced with nothingness. For can we not compare this thin atmospheric layer to nothingness? The distance between essence and existence is no wider.

Despair is a mortal failure. In our allegory it corresponds to the plane crashing to the ground. But the thinker who has been able to control his panic during his dizzying plunge, who has been able to "land smoothly" on the solid ground of being, has won the gamble: he has lost the illusion that the Nothingness which supported him is something real.

After the vertigo, essence offers a kind of shelter flooded with light, in which all the basic elements of life are found.

Epilogue

1. *"Sine qua non" of being*

If existence came before being, the integral human being would never "be." In him, by definition, essence is primary. Animals do exist prior to being, and their essence comes solely from their relationship to man. In the same way, it has been said that man "is" only through his relationship to God, which would have led to the conclusion that his existence also precedes his essence.

According to the story of Genesis, anyway, things existed prior to man, whereas man did not exist prior to God. The chief rebuttal to this is that the thing is an object for man, but that man is not an object for God. Thus the relationship between the thing and man is one of object to subject, while that between man and God is one of subject to subject. We can imagine a special relationship between two beings possessing the same characteristic as subjects.

In man, therefore, essence must precede existence, or man would be dehumanized. Essence is the *sine qua non* of his being. If we tried to reduce him to his existence, the being would never "be."

2. *The being that "is" (in the plain sense)*

We have pointed out the difficulty of defining being, since neither symbols, concepts, nor myths fully translate its richness. Is it a solution to say that man is spiritual energy, as the atom could be defined by the energy of its protons? No—for the human being is indefinable, since he is the image of the infinite. We will use the verb *to be* in speaking of him, specifying that it is used in the plain sense: man is a being who "is."

3. *Does nonbeing have a meaning?*

Heidegger discovered the "meaning" of being, and did not try to give a meaning to nonbeing. Why?

Because nothingness is a contradiction in terms.

4. *Hierarchy of essence*

Essence could be defined as a foundation, a unity, a persistence. Hartmann called it the *telos* of becoming. None of these formulas appeals to us. To us, essence is something imponderable. It is not, strictly speaking, the raw material of being, but being itself. It is the process by which things have a being (that which enables them to exist), and by which they are distinguished from one another.

All reality is therefore imbued with essence. There is, however, a kind of hierarchy of essences (and of existences, for that matter, as we saw). To go from the being of things to the world, from the world to existence, from existence to man, from man to being, from being to the soul, and from the soul to God is like climbing a ladder. Therefore, things are essence only in relation to man, who himself is essence only in relation to God. And in this need for an essence, which gives the *ens* the possibility of being, lies the difference between the human being and the Creator Being.

On the Act of Being

Conditions Necessary to the Act of Being

In order for a being to be, it is necessary for the "being in potentiality" to become a "being in act." Being is not reduced to the latent capacity for existing: this capacity must be realized in action. We must live our existence, that is, take on the material shape of our person and avail ourselves of the worldly things surrounding us. It is death that will realize once and for all, all the potentialities of essence, and will bring forth a new being of a higher degree: the pure essence-being, wholly integrated at the cost of the supreme sacrifice.

1. *Distance from the Being*

We consider essence to be the distance that separates God from man, and existence as the distance that separates man from the world.

Based on these definitions, we can use the concept of essence as a tool in the search for being. But it must be explained that even if no one is there to use this tool, essence already has a meaning in itself that is unique.

As for the notion of distance, is it still usable when it is a question of an infinite distance? Certainly—and for that matter, the distance that separates the Creator from man is really infinite, for that which separates man from the world may be expressed in finite terms, despite the reflection of infinity that still clings to the human being.

In the part entitled "The Being and the World," we will see what the world would be without man, which is a way of measuring the difference between these two terms. Here, we are trying to rediscover the foundation of the being that became man by studying the distance between it and the absolute Being. It is beyond that mysterious, grandiose interval that being "is."

Creation sprang from being like a light radiating from a fireplace. But while we see the light, its source remains beyond the range of our perception. Likewise, essence is ineffable and incomprehensible to the man-being.

The flames of creation, cooled by the very distance, allowed this inviting place, the world—in which the man-being was formed—to take shape. But the man-being is an existence-being, and only his death can take him back across the radiant zone separating the creature from the Absolute Being. As for the nature of this separation zone, it is everything we imagine it to be and more. It contains that which constitutes our being and justifies our creation. It is the mystery that the human spirit confronts.

2. *I am my being*

I am as a result of my being; that is, my being enables me to be what I am.

My being is therefore both the cause and the origin of my self. Yet it is my self that carries out the function of being. Why not equate my being with my capacity to be, then? Indeed, I am a being, and that being "is" only because it can carry out the function of being.

However, this capacity to be is both the result of the being that surges within me and the cause of my being, my principle-being. Nevertheless, we can distinguish several stages between essence and existence, but in the end, all of them lead only to the formation of a single being, the integral being. Futhermore, I am my being, without it being necessary that my existence should manifest itself. But even leaving existence aside, if I say, "I am my being," I fully define myself.

In other words, I am my being, independent of the existential man that I also am. But as the being by which I exist is both "me" and "mine," that being is in every way bound up with myself: my being *is* me. We cannot separate the principle and the cause of my self as pure being, but only as existential being. Likewise, we cannot separate my being from its capacity to be, as separate moments in the process of creating a being that becomes man. Indeed, it is by realizing this capacity to be that I "am," and it becomes impossible to separate being from the capacity to be.

According to G. Marcel, I am a being only if I succeed in creating a subject which precedes that being. We might object that this subject is not a subject, but another being. For if behind man lies being, behind being lies the Creator. It is therefore necessary to take a further step, and to conclude: it is because of God that I am.

To say that man is a being is not to say, "It is not man who is, but being"; for existence is thus irreparably separated from essence. In reality, when we say, "I am a being," we mean, "I exist as a being."

3. *The act of being and music*

Introducing music into a discussion as fundamental as that of being may appear odd indeed. Are not the mute depths of being completely ignorant of the sounds created by man?

But indeed, music is a "creation"; that is, it "is" relative to the musician who creates it, as man "is" relative to his Creator.

Hence, in order to explain the degree to which man *is* being, one might well say that it is in the same degree to which the sonata *is* the musician.

4. *Being and subjectivity*

Is subjectivity a reality in its relationship to being, or does the objective world hold being in its power? Can the being-in-the-world attain pure subjectivity? It is often misunderstood (both by those who deny it and by those who defend it to the death) because it springs from the depths of being, before being something in its own right. According to the classic definition of idealism, it is the quality of that which concerns the subject (but exclusively the subject).

We think, on the other hand, that it does not concern the subject exclusively. It is related to essence, and, fundamentally, to the principle-being. The subject, for that matter, is only the manifestation of this principle, and therefore it comes after essence. Subjectivity, therefore, is more a manifestation than a quality to us. Unlike the spiritualists, we do not consider it as outside of being and separate from objective man. Unlike the existentialists, we do not deny it, but rather recognize in it the force that springs from the depths of being.

Subjectivity is the crystallization of the indefinable force which man feels in himself, but cannot understand; it is a state of being. And it is in fulfilling the act of being that man becomes conscious of the subjective emanations of his soul.

5. *The sensation of being*

Without really knowing why or how, man intuitively experiences the sensation of being. This intuition is of crucial importance, and has served as a basis for certain philosophies.

But the act of being cannot be classified as an intellectual act; the sensation of being itself comes after it, just as consciousness of self comes after that sensation. Being "is," and the act of being accompanies it. It is from their dual reality that the sensation of being arises. From this we can conclude that they develop within themselves the intimate necessity of consciousness of self, with, as a further consequence, the consciousness of existing as a human being.

The basis of consciousness is above all the categorical necessity of knowing what I am; it is inherent in the human spirit, which without it would be completely animalistic. Nonetheless, the sensation of being and the consciousness of what one is are both a function of the primary act of being. This act, however, would remain a pure abstraction if man were not at the same time a man and an existing human. The conditions of his life (such as matter or the world) are therefore a requirement of the principle-being. Without them, the unique being would never be existential.

6. *The act of being*

How can consciousness help us to solve the mystery of being, at least in part? We will find it more in the realm of "sensation" than in that of intellect. I sense that I am before knowing what I am, and this tangible knowledge resists all the most logical arguments.

The act of being takes place at the level of essence, not that of intellect. It is clothed in such simplicity that all people perceive that they are, although they do not understand why. They are open to the simple truth "I am."

But the word "being" has too many possible meanings for the drama of the act of being not to have a need for knowledge and understanding of what I am. Thus, why not apply to being Pascal's statement about the heart and say that "it has its reasons which reason knows not of"? I am the being that I am and can conceive of no other.

Nonetheless, it is possible to distinguish three facets of being. One represents the act of being, which I accomplish as an integral being. The second shows that I am a subject, with my own individual characteristics. As for the third, it is the conscious certainty that "I am." In any case, the contrast between the capacity to be and the difficulty of understanding the being of "what is" remains strong.

Unlike man, inert matter, although also a reality, does not fulfill the act of being, because it is not capable of becoming conscious either of itself or of that act of being. A stone's way of being is merely to exist. Man "is," because he possesses both essence and existence, and because he consciously fulfills the act of being. The act of being and the consciousness of being are so closely tied that one may as well give up trying to distinguish between them.

7. *Analysis of the act of being*

The nature of the substratum of being was studied by G. Marcel in connection with the term 'act of being'.[1] The juxtaposition of these two terms poses a problem: are we to conceive of a subject (being) that fulfills the *act* of being, and which therefore "is," distinct from and prior to the act in question? Or should this subject be identified with its act, hence viewed as a "creation of self by self"?

The same problem is posed in regard to the act of existing. Is the

---

[1] *The Mystery of Being*

existing subject the act of existing in the process of creating itself? In any case, we come back to G. Marcel's formula, "I can speak of the act of being only if I refuse to consider anything resembling a subject"—a formula that necessarily implies a certain gap between my *ego* and my life.

And what might that "gap" consist of? Does being as pure essence become *a* being at the very moment that it becomes existent? Or is it a nothingness that makes itself what it is? And can this difference between my *ego* and my life really be reduced to the difference that exists between my self and my being?

G. Marcel asks in this regard whether or not one can experience oneself as "being" and as "existing" by a similar process. Quoting Charles du Bos, who expresses the "mysterious sentiment of the presence and distance of the soul at each hour of our life," he concludes, "While it is true that I am aware of my existence, my being, on the other hand, cannot be an object of awareness for me." But was G. Marcel not bowing to the existentialist reflex when he declined to recognize the reality of essence as such?

We are in fact so tied to existence that we cannot separate it from our being. For us, existence is a step forward that being takes as a result of the act of creation. The history of the being that becomes man is an ascent that continues independently of temporal episodes and in ignorance of such solutions of continuity. Man goes from essence to existence without being permitted to perceive the passage. Hence, of course, the temptation to deny the reality of essence in favor of existence alone. But such a denial is tantamount to rejecting the very vocation of the human essence, that of remaining intact through eternity, even after the end of existence. The destiny of each person is an unbroken ascent from his creation to his entrance into the light that attracts him.

Essence is the principle of beings. Possessing essence, I am destined to become a being subject to existence, then death. The tragedy of being unfolds both before and after life, and existence is only a twist in the plot. I am necessarily being before I am existence, but as being, I am inevitably man, that is to say, both spirit and matter.

For it is precisely the tension between being (made existent) and the objective world that gives rise to man. He is man only because he is existent, living, and made of matter. But his vocation is to triumph over the world and to continue, after death, to be that being which emerged into life. We should remember that this being became man only as a result of essence, which is spiritual principle and momentum. Also as a result of essence, this same being could become a subject. We can therefore reply to G. Marcel that it is not the subject that performs the act of being, and that he himself is not the subject.

It may be appropriate here to quote the phrase of Paul cited by Marcel: "Man is not himself and is not in oneself." This is equivalent to: "He exists in the world, and only the Being *is*." If it is God who creates man, man is more in God than in himself. Only God has the capacity to "be" with an infinite richness.

In his comments on "I am," G. Marcel abandons Descartes' self-assured tone. His *cogito* is tempered "by humility, fear, and wonderment." After all, do I not risk losing the gift of being by becoming unworthy? And yet, what a paradox, to tremble at losing something which I am not certain is real!

The word "wonderment" seems to us a trifle forced. To be sure, this gift brings light with it, but we cannot believe that it is light itself. How could our self be such, since it emerges in us by a process which we are not even permitted to understand? We manage only to be a faint reflection of light, if that word is taken to stand for the whole of creation. It is the Creator who gives man his capacity to be. Man not only exists in relation to God; he "is" in relation to God.

To define somehow this minimal difference between essence and existence, let us take the example of two thoughts that interfere with one another. An autistic thought happens to interrupt the flow of our ideas; we greet it rapidly; it goes away, and our attention returns to its main object. This occurs quite frequently, to the point that we no longer notice it. And yet we cannot think two things at the same time. Therefore, we are forced to admit that there is a certain gap between these two thoughts. In a similar way, a person absorbed by existence can become inattentive to essence, the consciousness of which sometimes surges within him. The existentialists seem to ignore this dual aspect of man, dwelling on his existential aspect and avoiding the problem of his being, his essence.

The living person exists. At his death he ceases to be a person and becomes a being. But death, which destroys the human in the being, does not reduce the being to nothingness; rather, it creates it as pure being. It should not be considered as an end, but as the threshold of a nonexistential life.

8. *Considerations on the statement "I am"*

Only God can say, "I am who I am," for only He has perfection—that is, the capacity to be fully and absolutely what He is.

The human "I am" is, however, a committing statement: I identify myself as no one other than myself, despite my resemblance to others, who also "are." I am my existence, but never all that I am; in order to exist, one must already be something.

I am what I am as spirit, but not in an absolute way, because I am not able to be fully what I might be, because I am a contingent being, because I am the prisoner of my being. I do not hope to know myself completely, for I am also what I am not—that is to say, what I am not yet.

Therefore, I do not know what I am. This does not prevent my consciousness-of-being, which is combined with being in a single chord, and that is but one with being itself, independent of self-knowledge.

Being and Existence

Preliminary Remarks

1. *Prayer and awareness*

Sleep is a time of reduced awareness.

Upon awakening, the human reflex is to pray. What a brilliant affirmation of being!

2. *Being and existence*

Just as there is no heat without fire, there is no existence without essence. In the unity of being and existence, where does one begin and the other end? While existence is something made and limited, being is not made (it is *created* by God), and is infinite: as a being in potentiality, it exists prior to everything. To be born—that is, to become existent—is merely to "appear" and to end the state of potentiality.

At the end of time, being will reveal itself to matter, and matter will reassume its true role: to be a docile tool in the hands of the human being, although it subjugated him during his earthly existence, even if

65

man is capable of transforming or even disintegrating it. However, despite his emancipation from matter, the human being, merged with the Supreme Being, will nonetheless retain his individuality, joined to the consciousness of his unique nature.

3. *Metaphysics of why and how*

"Why am I on earth?" is an agonizing and eternal question. It is a question that pertains to metaphysics, the question of man who wishes to raise his spirit above matter.

It has an answer: every being in potentiality, preexisting in the divine will, must necessarily enter the world. But in addition to the "why" of existence, there is the "how" of existence: from what was being created? From air, wind, or light? Is it matter or nothingness?

The original reality of being was the divine essence itself. While it differs from that essence, after all, the being retains a resemblance to God, as though the Creator had wanted to see Himself in it, like a face is a more or less faithful mirror.

Because he was created, man wonders about creation. And thus he cannot conclude that he is nothingness, for nothingness is no more capable of the act of questioning than of any other act. The very notion of an act is tied to that of being. We conclude, therefore, that if the Being *exists* as man, man *is* as a being.

Being and Existing

1. Possibility of an essence without existence

Bergson proved the impossibility of nothingness in these terms: "If I say Object A does not exist, what I mean first of all is that one might think that Object A exists. Yet how can one think about Object A without thinking that it exists? Therefore, by the very fact that I say 'Object A,' I attribute to it a kind of existence, were it that of a mere possible, i.e., a pure idea."

In reasoning from this brilliant statement, we see that an object may be in an idea and yet not exist, materially. But rather than use the Bergsonian term "kind of existence," we prefer to speak of something that possesses essence but not existence. For if a (mental) reality can be something that does not exist, is this not proof that there is an essence even outside of existence?

Bergson also asks, "What difference can there be between the idea of existing Object A and the pure and simple idea of Object A?" The answer, we say, is different depending on whether it is a question of any object or of man. For a material object existing in the world, the difference is nil. But man is not only existence: before existing in the world, man "is"; he may "be" without existing, not only as someone else's mental image, but because he possesses an essence that gives him his reality, apart from his coming into existence.

If one defines man as the being in its totality, we see that Bergson's argument cannot apply to him, for the master's thought was limited to the existence-being. It shows us, at least, that to conceive of the being apart from existence is not an absurdity.

G. Marcel cites another example of a similar nature when he speaks of a past thing and states that it continues to "be" in a certain sense, though it has already ceased to exist. As with regard to the "Object A" posited by Bergson, we cannot say that it "exists," because its existence is already over. But is this not a new case of being without a definite existence, and of essence entirely devoid of existence?

From there it is only a further step to the human soul. What is it after man's death? It *is*, without existing, and "is" independent of the imagination. For "Object A" (a three-headed man, for example) "is" only because of man's imagination. That imagination, because it is superimposed on the world, can to some extent restore being to something that no longer exists. Why is it, however, that some people stubbornly reject the possibility of being without existing, apart from the world of imagination? Essence is the cause, not the effect, of imagination. And if we assume that essence can dispense with existence, we confirm the precedence of the former over the latter.

2. *Why must I be before I exist*

We must consider the consciousness of being and the consciousness of existing as two separate, successive phenomena. The being that becomes man necessarily knows both states of consciousness, which may be compared to two levels of vision. In the act of seeing, I see (on the level of perception) because I possess the sensory organs of sight. Similarly, I exist because I possess essence. In both cases, there is a transition from the potency to the act, i.e., the use of a faculty.

Furthermore, does the thing man sees and the sight of that thing precede the faculty of sight? No, of course not. The faculty of sight is primary, since it permits me to perform the act of seeing. But consciousness of self may be compared to the faculty of sight, which would imply, by analogy, that essence is primary over existence. Man "is" not because he exists, but exists because he "is" (since he "is" before he exists), and he becomes aware of his existence only because he is conscious of his essence; existence is the means by which consciousness of self is objectified.

In short, essence and our consciousness of it are prior to and primary over existence and our consciousness of it.

3. *Dialectic of essence and existence*

Why is contemporary philosophy so interested in the problem of existence? Is it because man is more interested in the world than ever, now that he has penetrated some of its mysteries? Is it because one would rather make less of an effort in thinking (because existence is easy to understand)? Is it because one enjoys thinking of oneself as an individual, and differentiating oneself from others? We should not forget, however, that only essence truly gives man his individual character, his consciousness, his life. Only essence goes deep, and it is the surface that draws our attention.

Thus, the death of a beloved person creates in us the feeling of emptiness in the existential realm. The more our love was attached to a look, a face, a shape, whose absence we mourn, the greater is our sadness; it was a body that enabled us to feel an existential presence. But a stronger love can be experienced on the level of essences. Relationships between spirits make unions deeper than relationships between bodies. And essence remains after death, so that the true love is a love that does not die.

4. *Ontological inaccuracies of existentialism*

The object of existential philosophy is being in its human aspect. Its ontology may be defined as the study of the deep roots of being, but of the being that has become man. G. Marcel, for example, was aware of this duality, for he wrote: "The more we lay stress on the object as such...the more we shall be obliged to leave its existential aspect in darkness."[1] He stresses the value of this "sensible presence of the thing which, if it is not confused with its existence, seems...as

---

[1] *The Mystery of Being*, pp. 26-27.

though it were...its most immediate revelation.... I think the effect of the reservation is to keep a sort of gap or interval between something which may be the being of existence or which may simply be its appearance."[2] But elsewhere, he seems to take a different position: "To think of existence is ultimately to think of the impossibility of any opposition here between being and appearance."[3] Whence his formula, the loftiness of which is admirable: "The existent is at the same time a thing and yet in some way more than a thing."[4]

Yet a certain confusion prevails among these thoughts of Marcel's, and we can detect in it traces of confusion between essence and existence: what is the "palpable presence of the thing" of which he speaks, if not a reflection of essence? Then why not separate, in man, the spirit as the incarnate reality of the immaterial Spirit, from the spirit as opposed to matter? We think it is essential to clearly distinguish essence from existence, and to stop thinking of them as a single reality.

In our view, existence is man's ability to "be" materially in the world, that is, to live. As for essence, it also implies life, but is still something else entirely; for to be is to deploy our essence independently of matter. However, since we must "be" as beings existing in the world, we risk losing sight of the fact that we exist only because we possess a being. Therefore, it is better to replace G. Marcel's "I am my body" with "I am my being," since it is my being that serves as a foundation for my body.

G. Marcel for his part underlined the ambiguity of the word existence. He was able to extract the difference between the existence of things and that of being: "the existence of the thing as a thing" is not "nonbeing" but rather "just short of being." However, he remains under the spell of existentialist thought when he says: "Existence appears to us, at best, as necessarily identical to being in its authenticity." In fact, we think of the demands of being as related to essence, and not to existence.

Let us recall here that poetic image of Rilke, quoted by G. Marcel: "We are the bees of the invisible. We madly raid the honey of the

---

[2] *Ibid.*

[3] *The Mystery of Being*, p. 28.

[4] *The Mystery of Being*, p. 29.

visible, to store it in the great golden hive of the invisible."[5] The philosopher concludes from the poet: "...every human being...shares in this activity...by which the visible is transmuted into the invisible."[6] In our act of living, we gamble with essence, and we crystallize it in thousands of acts performed in the course of existence; but essence is inexhaustible, while existence (earthly life) will disappear.

G. Marcel refuses both to define being as a kind or as a modality of essence, for "we shall run the risk of thinking that existence is a sort of specification of a fundamental act; which act would be the act of being."[7] Existence, indeed, is neither a mode nor a specific form of being, since it is through its very union with essence that it forms the integral human being. We wish to recall the real precedence of essence over existence (not precedence in the temporal sense, of course, so that we can accept them as concomitant). But having said this, we come to a conclusion rather Marcelian in its formulation: man achieves the fusion of essence and of existence.

---

[5] *The Mystery of Being*, p. 33.

[6] *Ibid.*

[7] *Ibid.*

Existence and Life

1. *Living, being, and existing*

The human being may be studied in his three possible manifestations: his being, his existence, and his life. In fact, these three aspects are so closely related that some contemporary philosophers have tried to reduce them to a single one. G. Marcel first considers existence, which he views as preceding essence; I live before I am.

A paradoxical position, which ties man's reality more to existence than to essence, while apparently forgetting the notion of freedom. Is the obligation to live compatible with freedom, which is the very stamp of essence?

a) What *is* existing?

To exist is to place oneself in the world. But conversely, the world is existential only for man; indeed, without him it would be only an infinitely tiny ball, lost in the vast spaces, meaningless. Only man can give it a meaning, by becoming conscious of his position in space and time, which are human notions. The problem of time is always agonizing for man, even after Einstein's researches in relativity. Is time not made up of crumbs from a larger time, and should space not be fragmented into however many spatial frameworks in which matter moves? Could time depend on matter, which itself depends on space?

In any event, man must escape from that contingent prison which is the universe, of which he has no need in order to "be."

b) What *is* living?

To live is likewise to be in the material world, but to develop in it, and to move toward a goal. The body and the spirit, each in its path, go in search of being.

c) What *is* being?

To define being is the very task of philosophy, and it is the thinker's most arduous problem, even if he has tried to divide it by distinguishing being from being and the capacity to be. For has not the non-philosopher lost the notion of being after having been submerged in existence and driven solely by the desire to live?

Before living or existing, we *are*, and it is essence which enables us to be what we are, giving us our individuality and our personality. Essence is often compared to light, but it is a light that cannot be seen; it is all the more dazzling compared to the dullness of matter. But what would become of man if the light of his essence did not combat the darkness of his nothingness? He would be a prey to anguish and despair. Yet sometimes he chooses to alienate himself from himself and to identify with darkness, nothingness and death.

The principle of man's life is his essence, which was given to him by God. It alone can save him, it alone enables him to exist, to live and to be. But can we not reply that, to the contrary, essence burns much too hotly to allow existence to coexist with it? Is it not rather like volcanic lava, which destroys life on the mountain that has grown up because of it? Perhaps. But we should recall the myth of the Titan, who symbolizes man. Does not its strength consist of maintaining a balance between its essence and its existence, of preventing the latter from choking the former, without being destroyed by its fire?

2. *Shadows and light in life*

The play of light and shadow have a poetic charm for us, for they are the image of what we experience in continually passing from the nontemporal to the material. The "sweet kingdom of Earth," as Bernanos said, has its enchanting aspects. It is the stage on which man plays his part. It is the place where man finds that love which delights and wounds him.

3. *Contingencies and cerebralism*

Contingencies in life might be tolerable, but imagination makes them more frightening in their aspect. Thus, man is afraid of the unknown, fearful of tomorrow and of a thousand unforeseen ills. He creates his own tragic vision of the future. Certain existential fears of the future are even hysterical at times, accompanied by anguish, terror, and despair.

Man can save himself from this fear of life through worship of the Being, for the roots of being go to the deepest parts of essence, and can transmit consciousness of the essential, like a nourishing sap. There is nothing that cannot become creative, even the thought of Death, which is so violent to our reason.

4. *Defense of death*

Man feels the specter of death drawing closer to him each day. It is inevitable, and one can speak of its necessity. But it is necessary not only for fulfillment of the essence-being; it is also a moral brake on the temptations of existence. For if the web of a life can be broken suddenly, there have also been lives wasted simply because no one dreamed of putting them to use.

What would life be without death? What meaning, even, would an endless life have, even an apparently happy one? It would be like a rough copy full of errors, and would never become that clearly defined act on which death rests like a seal. An immortal human being would be a Sisyphus, weary of life and of himself. And civilizations, like people, would lose all vitality if the rhythm of history were no longer measured by successive generations. If, for example, the Roman empire had continued to our time, humanity would not have benefited from the medieval and modern discoveries. New ideas arise from the decline of the old, and "the old is father to the new." In other words, death calls to life; it is death that permits the creation of new beings, thus helping to give value to the Being.

5. *Bergson's Object A (continued)*

Bergson, as we saw, proves the difference between essence and existence by the possibility of imagining an "Object A" that does not exist.

But the proof would be just as correct if it were done in reverse. There are things which "are," which we are unable to imagine. Example: the soul, the spirit, the being. Thought, indeed, capitulates when it tries to portray being; the intellect is silent.

St. Augustine said, "If thou knowest not thyself, know at least that it is beautiful to know oneself, for the soul is all life."

If we can imagine that which is not, and if we cannot imagine that which is, the reason is that the capacity for thought comes not from existence, but from the Being.

6. *Feeling of existence and feeling of essence*

To Heidegger, man is unfinished; hence his anguish. To us, the existence that characterizes man is precisely that which puts the finishing touch on essence, at the risk of overshadowing it. Anguish is merely a reaction against that neglect, a need to search for essence, which comes from a command of the Creator.

Being, Thought, and Nothingness

Thought

1. *Thought as an outgrowth of being*

The act of thinking is like an outgrowth of being. It is a point of contact between man and being, and serves as a conduit to being. But at the same time, it is an elevation of matter to the search for a meaning, an ascent of existence toward essence. Existence cannot suffice for man. If life, for example, offers reflections of beauty, essence is Beauty itself.

Conscious thought tries to bridge this gulf between essence and existence. It is a kind of emissary of being; for it is consciousness of essence that is primary in man, and is then transformed into consciousness of existence, permitting contact between those two worlds. Thus, a person who has no consciousness of himself cannot think, but if he were deprived of essence, he could not have consciousness of himself. Thus, the conscious being occupies a kind of threshold between the depths of being and those of superficial existence, which permits a kind of plunge toward the deepest parts of essence.

2. *The essence of thought*

Thought is what enables man to analyze things and to analyze himself. But can it also be analyzed? Will man need to use other faculties in order to know thought, or can thought think about itself? How is it defined?

It is an emanation of the inner forces of being, emerging from its inner core as light comes from the sun. Access to it is therefore as difficult as to the being from which it emanates; since its origins and causes must remain unknown to us, we are forced to study it through its external manifestations. Could such a superficial analysis permit a thorough knowledge of it? Is it not tantamount to describing a process whose secret eludes us?

We can at least uncover its main characteristics. Thought, for example, has great rapidity; it is so fast that it may be compared to light. Being, which generates it, cannot slow it down, and man receives it (without having anything to do with it). He organizes it, but does not create it, and at times is just barely aware of it. Thus, even if man thinks, thought remains a mystery to him in its essence, just as the act of seeing remains incomprehensible to him and yet he sees. We might say it is being that not only thinks for him, but guides his thoughts and leaves him thinking blindly. Thought, therefore, has something in common with emotion: it owes to being something more than its mere birth.

It did not escape Nietzsche that consciousness grasps only a portion of our thoughts. But he did not go so far as to conclude that if the thought not grasped by consciousness is reduced to nothingness, it is from failure to become existential. Real thought is indeed like a crystallization of essence within existence. If we compare being to a volcano, conscious thoughts are solidified lava; others are wisps of smoke that evaporate. This accumulated lava is a remainder in the world of the existence of that mysterious world of being from which they emerged.

Being and Nothingness

1. *Nothingness and creation*

The problem which man has struggled with throughout the ages, the real reason for his anguish, is "to be or not to be."

Bergson helped to pose this problem with the aid of analogies. For example, the being/nothingness dichotomy might be compared to the order/disorder dichotomy. Disorder has no definite meaning in the realm of creation; it is merely "the order we are not seeking." This formula tries to show that nothingness does not precede being. It consists merely of an idea in man's mind, and disappears before being, which *is* a reality. This reality is seen by a person who is capable of looking inside himself, whereas the existence of nothingness has not been proved, nor has its essence been defined. And while being may to some extent be the object of physical experiences, Bergson compares nothingness to the absolute void which has never been experienced: "It would have boundaries, it would have contours, it would therefore still be something. But in reality, there is no void. We can perceive, and in fact can conceive only of substance. Something disappears only because something else replaces it."

We cannot imagine being and nothingness at the same time. Once being prevails, nothingness is destroyed.

But since being was created, can we not imagine nothingness as that which "was" before the creation of being? In fact, God is the creator of being. In all logic, therefore, He should also be the creator of nothingness! We should recognize, rather, that nothingness is symbolic. It is merely a product of man's imagination as he tries to understand creation. Before being, there was no "nothingness"; there was God, who created everything in His image, and thus created only beings. It is in this way that nothingness could have a being, and to speak of the creation of nothingness would be absurd; it is being that God created.

2. *Being and the All*

Man is; he is conscious both of his existence and of his essence as spirit. But if the Spirit "is," it is All, and there can be no nothingness, for in being all, it is everywhere. It travels throughout space, with space and time as inseparable companions, and it spreads across the cosmos, scattering light where there was darkness, and music where silence reigned. Being is omnipresent, in things, animals, and people; it is being which enables them to be transformed. Being rules alone, for the merest presence of nothingness would imply the non-existence of being, and consequently of all. It would be natural, therefore, never to call the being anything but the All. However, if everything exists, how could nothingness coexist with the totality of its opposite?

3. *Nothingness and Nothing*

On the other hand, if being is all, nothingness can only be nothing. How could we image nothingness without being? "Silence cannot be imagined without noise, nor darkness without light," wrote St. Augustine.

If nothingness is (as a virtual reality), it "is" by virtue of being. And if nothingness exists in thought, it does so because being exists in reality. However, to accept the existence of nothingness and of being at the same time would be to say that a thing can be and not be at the same time. However, since the Being is being, it cannot be nothingness at the same time. Therefore, nothingness does not exist.

4. *Incoherence of the Notion of nothingness*

Whereas Hegel contrasts the idea of nothingness to that of being as thesis to antithesis, Sartre writes: "Negation will never be derived from being. The necessary condition for our saying *not* is that nonbeing be a perpetual presence in us and outside of us, that nothingness haunt being."[1] The argument Sartre uses to defend the thesis of the reality of nonbeing seems questionable to us. Indeed, it appears paradoxical and contradictory that nothingness, considered as a perpetual presence, should derive from negation, whereas being, likewise a perpetual presence, should derive from affirmation. This argument leads to positing a being and a nothingness devoid of essence, since their foundation is merely the result of human activity (whereas by definition, being is an essence created by God).

Moreover, how can we tolerate the idea that nothingness haunts being, and admit that the real can emerge only from their fusion? This fusion is in fact nothing but a confusion. The philosophy of being must reject this compromise with nothingness, which would imply first its negation, then its destruction. Furthermore, the proof that nonbeing has neither reality nor value is that it has no peculiar characteristics, since it must borrow them from being while turning them inside out. It seems inconceivable to us that being and nothingness should cooperate in establishing the real: in effect, nonbeing can be only a useless tool, since it does not exist, and since, on the other hand, the creative being is self-sufficient.

In answer to the question, "What was there before there was a world?" Sartre states: "What we deny today, we who are established in being, is what there was of being before this being."[2] But if he thus rejects a being before the world-being, can he really be sure that he does not accept nothingness? He extricates himself by concluding that "before" and "nothingness" are only retroactive ideas, and we

---

[1] *op. cit.*, p. 11.

[2] *op. cit.*, p. 16.

conceive of them only because the after and the real exist. In fact, what he offers as a working hypothesis, as a concept created by man in accordance with his own situation, is nothingness. This does not hold for the notion of "before." It existed prior to man. If there were nothing before being, from what could man have emerged? On the other hand, if there were something before, that something had to be a being. Therefore, we must not now deny that there was a being before the being that we are.

As for the "original void," if we consider it as something other than a void of this world, and as "before" this world, we end up with "a total indetermination which it would be impossible to conceive, even and especially as a nothingness."[3] In effect, the empty being or Sartre's nothingness have no consistency; therefore, they cannot exist, either with being, or before it. And this argument leads us also to the conclusion that nothingness does not exist; nonbeing is not even an *a posteriori*.

We pointed out the twofold impossibility of considering nonbeing as a product of being and as a concomitant reality of being. It is equally impossible for us to imagine nonbeing as a reality subsequent to being, since nonbeing does not contain the qualities of "that which is." Furthermore, if nonbeing followed being, this would imply its own contingency, since, if there were no being, there would be no nonbeing either. How could nonbeing take on the negative outlines of being in the obscurity of the thought which conceives it? Nothingness can neither create nor cause anything to be created, not even a mental image; it cannot be created either, for that which is nothing can be neither the subject nor the object of a creative act.

Sartre's portrait of being has an extraordinary side, with its irrational brush strokes and nonexistent colors. But we are adamantly opposed to his presentation of nonbeing as an image reflected by the mirror of being. At most, it is only a caricature of it, like those given by distorting mirrors which make images gigantic or tiny. Even if we dub nonbeing "an aborted fetus of being," that term would still be incorrect, because it would give nonbeing a false reality. An equally incorrect comparison would consist of comparing nonbeing to the tiny atom in contrast to the vast cosmos. For after all, the atom is of

---

[3] *op. cit.*, p. 16.

the same nature as the universe and is made up of the same matter, while nonbeing is inconsistent and nonexistent compared to being. It is futile to use an image to make that which is nonexistent, existent.

5. *Respective situations of being and of nothingness*

With regard to the "essence" of being and of nothingness, let us now see if the reality of one cancels out the other, or if, on the other hand, it makes possible the other's reality. Can we think of them as two co-rulers, reigning together over the world of reality? Does each have its own realm—one, the objective world; the other, the subjective world? Are their powers compatible, and are they legitimate? If we are interpreting Sartre's thought correctly, two solutions can be visualized. Either being and nothingness appear and disappear simultaneously, or else being precedes nonbeing, which looms after it like a distorted shadow. We must recognize that there is a certain coherence in this second assumption: "It is from being that nonbeing takes its being." The disappearance of being would mean its disappearance, and nonbeing would, so to speak, be a whim of the fate of being, and would accompany it like a shadow. But Sartre forgets that the presence of this shadow would hamper the freedom of being like Sisyphus's rock, since being could never get rid of it.

Even if we assume, as he does, that being precedes nonbeing since a shadow cannot exist unless an object is illuminated, let us examine what happens to the object without its shadow and to the shadow without its object. If being "is" not, could nonbeing be its negation? Why does Sartre make being and nonbeing mutually interdependent? As though being might need its negation!

Nonbeing cannot be viewed as the negation of being without recognizing the impossibility of its coexistence with being. Perhaps, however, the nonbeing thesis might be partially accepted for the period preceding the existence of being. Being can then be considered as an absence of being (before its existence) and also as a kind of existence (as the possibility of becoming existent). It is in this hypothetical state that being could have gone through the experience of nonbeing. But in conclusion, we always come back to the precedence of being over this supposed nonbeing, which would mean the destruction of being. Therefore, in the name of the supreme reality of being, we eliminate the shadow of nonbeing.

Furthermore, we cannot accept a coexistence of being and nonbeing, for no system mentions a conflict between those two notions; however, their opposition would be inevitable, since nonbeing by definition implies the abolition of being, and any "peaceful coexistence" between them is unthinkable. In addition, an essential characteristic of being is to be unique, which rules out the presence of nonbeing. Consequently, we must reject any system that assumes the coexistence of being and of nonbeing.

6. *The state of absence*

The notion of absence can clarify may things when it is used in place of the ideas of negation and of nonbeing. If we assume that a being may be in a state of absence, we will better understand what nothingness and death signify.

What, indeed, is death, if not the absence of life? And what is space, if not the absence of matter? Likewise, nothingness may be conceived of as an absence of being. The term absence applies to the existential realities; thus, the negation never applies to more than one being at a time. It does not attack the Being, whose reality is dazzling, and whose strength overflows to such an extent that He communicates a kind of reality to His own negation! In any case, negations would never acquire any reality except a mental one. But they can influence the human mind, induce it to deny itself while contradicting itself in endless searches for truth. In face of the world, in face of his being, man feels the need to attach himself to something which can conquer his anguish, and, if necessary, nullify it. If he lived in a world less tied to matter, he might not perhaps have this need to create the illusion of nothingness, this taste for meeting death halfway—death, the great inspiration of poets.

By a similar process, hate, for example, which at first is only the absence of love, can take on an existence of its own, in the sense that it would "be" even if there were no love. However, death, the absence of life, is conceivable only from the standpoint of the living being. And the illusory vertigo in the presence of space, the terror with regard to the infinite and the realms of Nothingness, comes from a purely human need to attach oneself to a twig so as not to be swallowed up by the real abysses, those of life and of being. It is his own being that makes man tremble with fear; he feels that he is called upon to live out the most tragic of tragedies, his thought goes astray in the infinite, and his feet, stuck in the ground, find the holes dug by his negations. How much more loyal would it be to say that neither death, nor nothingness, nor the infinite voids are something; they are nothing, for they are merely absence.

7. *Being in potentiality and nonbeing*

Eggenspieler[4] considered being in the act and being in potentiality as analogous. Guided by Aristotelian philosophy, he wrote that, according to the identity principle, "we posit being, on the one hand," and on the other hand, "nonbeing only," thus excluding potentiality, which becomes "an unintelligible notion." Potentiality has traditionally been defined as nonbeing in relation to being; logically, therefore, it cannot survive if the two entities are completely separated. When we posit being on the one hand, and nonbeing on the other hand, without any connection between them, there is no room left for potentiality. However, Aristotle tried to effect a synthesis between the Parmenidian thesis, which sees only being, and the Heraclitian thesis, which sees only nonbeing, by means of notion of potentiality.

"Nonbeing in relation to being"? Yes, but above all, potentiality is a "coming into being," not only being which has not yet reached a certain state. If being "is" not yet, it is what will be. Potentiality is, therefore, a becoming rather than a nonbeing. It is a future unfolding, before us, urging us to make it real in order to bring us close to being itself.

Conversely, we may say that nonbeing negates not only being, but potentiality as well. Only the notion of becoming leaves the latent being the possibility of being realized in the act. It is more positive than that of nonbeing, for it is already a step toward reality.

But if we now refer to another of his definitions ("synthesis of being and of nonbeing"), potentiality appears to be endowed with an un-

---

[4] *op. cit.*, pps. 11-12.

imaginable power, the power to integrate being and its negation, to synthesize a reality with that which nullifies it. It is better to go back to the statement that potentiality implies becoming. For the future is positivity; it permits a synthesis with what "is" not yet, but must be, whereas it cannot coincide with nonbeing.

The coexistence of being and of nonbeing within potentiality appears absurd, since the positivity of the one and the negativity of the other are incompatible. Our reasoning thus compels us to state that potentiality is closer to becoming than to nonbeing. For, like becoming itself, if it "is" not yet, it inevitably will be. Potentiality and nonbeing cannot be reconciled, because potentiality "is," being destined to be, and may be considered a faculty of being, the faculty of being what it will be.

8. *What being is not*

In G. Marcel's *Metaphysical Journal*,[5] the part concerning the essence of being does not satisfy us. Indeed, existentialism tries to reduce man to his existence, refusing to see the notion of being that rises in his consciousness.

Here and there we find formulas that bring us up short. For example: "I cannot state that being is; A is, B is, A participates in being, B also, but the being in which they participate is perhaps nothing of which we might say that it is." In our view, A participates in being while it is essence and existence, and it is being which enables it to exist. But being should not be confused with the act of being. Being would indeed be nothing if it were not realized completely; being reduced to itself, though that may seem paradoxical, "is" not: it must be realized in the act.

G. Marcel appears to confuse the verb *to be* with the noun *being*. To him essence "is" not if it is not mingled with existence. Thus, he thinks that if man did not exist, he would not be. To us, on the other hand, man would not exist if he "were" not, or at least, he would exist only as something dead. Likewise, to G. Marcel's argument that "A is because it exists," we reply, "A exists because it is." Hence, being must be in order to exist; it exists, therefore it "is."

---

[5] *op. cit.*, p. 104 and 111.

Being "is" as a spirit; it exists as man. Here it is necessary to quote G. Marcel: "Does not the solution consist of positing the omnipresence of being, and what I will perhaps improperly call the immanence of thought to being, that is, and therefore, that transcendence of being over thought?" But to judge being solely according to its omnipresence is to confuse being and the Being; one sins by excess. But when we define being in relation to thought, and by extension, in relation to thinking man, this time one sins by omission, because being is something more than thought; thought is only the expression of being.

Hence, to exercise the faculty of being would be to live a life in which time does not exist. However, to be is above all to live essentially in the richness of the moment, which, in Eggenspieler's words, transcends matter, the world and existence.

9. *Essence and nothingness*

Could essence be only a nothingness, that nothingness to which the existentialists try to reduce being? Does it amount to symbols? Has it neither substance nor shape? How, then, can the human mind grasp it?

And in the first place, why could the mind not visualize it as a being? Probably because it is the being of all beings. Since it is their very foundation, even in our mind, the mind cannot comprehend it in all its profundity. Essence is like an eruption of a flame of which we see only a pale glimmer. But let us borrow G. Marcel's analogy of music: can music be reduced to the notes and sounds that we perceive, and that remain ingrained in our memory? Doesn't this combination of chords appear to possess something more that constitutes their synthesis, that seems to be hidden behind them, and that is revealed to us by a kind of memory or regret preserved in us? Is it a nothingness that follows being? We said that nothingness was not even an *a posteriori*. But if a nothingness can be construed in the context of being, if a thing can become nothingness, its being must necessarily exist first. When the cycle of its existence is complete, the material thing is transformed into dust. Is that dust not equivalent to a kind of nothingness?

Lavoisier seems to have been quite optimistic in declaring that in nature "nothing is lost, nothing is created, everything is transformed." Our contemporaries ask, rather, what will remain of the universe at the end of the destructive process in which it is involved. Cosmic dust? Not even that! The vision of this destiny for the world can fill man with anguish, for it gives him the idea of a "nothingness." But what would that "nothingness" be? An infinite, a void, without shape or substance? In order to imagine it, man would have to be transported beyond matter through the use of his intellectual faculties. However, because he is human and therefore submerged in matter, he cannot master the cosmos and its infinite boundaries. It is, therefore, only by turning toward the depths of his soul that man can have a vague idea of matter reduced to less than dust, and can forge a concept of that kind of nothingness, which will never be anything but a pale reflection of the philosopher's nothingness.

Nothingness and Creation

1. *The unjustifiable notion of nothingness*

If man conceives of nothingness as an absolute, not only as the negative of being, he condemns himself to annihilation. How could man have an idea of nothingness, which excludes all possibility of conceiving an idea? Absolute nothingness would obliterate everything, including the notion of it. God created the heaven and earth, thought and man; He created everything, without having to create nothingness, or any other kind of infinite into which to fling the world. For the very idea of creation excludes that of nothingness; everything that is created is *ipso facto* a being. However, nothingness can neither "have a being" nor "be a being."

Even assuming that it were possible to create nothingness, why would God have created it? He was able to create space—a reality which may be considered as material—instantly. In any case, the created could not include nothingness, which would then lose its very characteristic of nonbeing. The expression "creation of nothingness" is antinomical—indeed, absurd.

2. *Nothingness and "Ens creatum"*

Man must seek himself as being-made-man. Only that choice allows him to assert his freedom, for to choose, in the Kierkegaardian sense, is to "gather" the deep meaning of the act of creation, that infinite that connects God and man. Opposite, there is only nothingness, not as a cause, but as an end, and as the destiny of the existent.

Heidegger, considering nothingness as an eternal law controlling the fate of matter, seems to contradict himself, since he sometimes conceives of man as not subject to the determinism of matter but as "self-determination," sometimes as a being "for death," with death seen in its absolute necessity. To him, man is a being-there, meaning that he is already there, thrown into the world; but no one threw him there and there is no reason for his presence. We cannot accept such an answer to the problem of creation, to the question of the origin of beings. It is a refusal to seek a cause, a flight from the problem at hand.

To be sure, we must begin with the present reality. Our presence, that of the Other, that of the world are unquestionable facts to us. Yet we have an origin, and why refuse to say that that origin is explained by a divine process, the process of creation? Man must choose between creation (which is principle) and nothingness (which is end). For we could not consider nothingness as a principle nor creation as an end (it necessarily precedes its extinction).

3. What was there before the creation of the cosmos?

Nothingness? No—there was God, and God alone. Indeed, nothingness could not inhabit the world before its creation, since there was nothing to inhabit, neither space nor matter. And nothingness is not what was there before the creation, but rather a creator. If nothingness existed, therefore, would it date from the creation? But why would God have created it? What would have been the need for it? Or the meaning of it? And if one replies that it is in order to lead being to its destruction once its destiny has been accomplished, one gives proof that nothingness is viewed much more as an anti-being than as a being.

Nothingness, Existence, Existentialism

1. *Consciousness of existence and nothingness*

If Hegelian time could be called a negation of the negation, nothingness is the negation of nothing: neither life, nor existence, nor being (the unassailable trinity, because its three parts "are," at the same time). Being, however, may be called the negation of nothingness, and nothingness may be called the darkness of darkness, reversing the Augustinian definition of truth (*Lumen de lumine*). This does not even give it a reality, for it is as impossible to attribute a being to nothingness as to imagine a thought without mind and a creation without a creator. If there is no effect without a cause, when there is no cause, there is no effect, either. Yet nothingness is neither cause nor effect; it exists only as a postulate, as a working hypothesis put forth by the mind in its search for itself; it may, to some extent, bring psychological comfort to the anguished man, anguish being a reaction to being. But even in imagination, nothingness cannot be considered a mental image, for if human intelligence could conceive of it, it would extinguish itself. Even in the world of ideas, if nothingness exists, the world disappears.

How then should nothingness ultimately be defined? It is the temptation of a consciousness that is impotent to comprehend being, but it draws no reality from the fact that being has one; it is neither in opposition to being, prior to being, nor after being; nor is it nonbeing. It is only that which "is" not, never was, never will be. It cannot serve as its own definition; we should not say, "It is nothingness," but must use the verb without a complement and say, "It 'is' not; only being 'is'." For the mere idea of being destroys the notion of nothingness.

2. Hume's system and nothingness

In Hume's *Treatise of Human Nature*, he bases one of his theses on the impossibility of infinitely dividing space and time. If space were infinitely divisible, graphically or numerically, one could never have the notion of unity, which is in opposition to that of divisibility. As a matter of fact, since such a reduction ad infinitum is inconceivable, we can conceive of unity. By thus denying the indefinite divisibility of space, Hume gives us an argument against the reality of nothingness. For unity is the characteristic of being, and it excludes the reality of a nothingness other than an imaginary one.

For, quite obviously, if being could be infinitely divided, everything would be reduced to nothingness. But is it conceivable that human thought should be able to divide and subdivide being until it is transformed into nothingness? Would that not be to accept being and nothingness simultaneously? Hume explains the impossibility of dividing space and time ad infinitum by the unity of being. To be sure, nothingness has no grip over it, but perhaps the human mind needs the antithesis in order to reach the synthesis, and it invented nothingness in order to become more aware of being? Could nothingness be a method of comprehension in reverse? But if white helps to understand black, and noise to understand silence, the light must not be darkened by shadow, nor the white blackened by darkness! Why not rather strive to directly grasp the idea itself? Is the mind a slave to antithesis? On the contrary, it is capable of attaining the infinite by its own forces, and should approach the problem of being without the absurd crutch of nothingness. To make a positive statement by way of negation is the sign of an imperfect mind. To define shadows by reference to light can be done. But the reverse operation, like the creation of a nothingness in order to imagine being, shows an impoverishment.

Consequently, full consciousness of self in man can eliminate the idea of nothingness, and restore the certainty of his existence. The temptation of nothingness is like an illness of bacterial origin; a healthy organism eliminates the virus itself. Thus, the notion of being naturally destroys the thought of nothingness, which is antagonistic to it.

Nothingness and Philosophical Systems

1. *The existentialist nothingness*

Existentialist philosophy opposes traditional philosophy in the way it conceives of nothingness.

E. Mounier notes that Sartre's predecessors considered nothingness a kind of negative object, thus giving it a certain substance, and even positing it as the substance of things. For his part, Sartre denies this characteristic of "substance," and states that the notion of nothingness simultaneously permits us to affirm and to deny being. Being and nonbeing are considered opposite manifestations of being. And yet Sartre also thinks that being comes out of nothingness and must return to it. For him, nothingness does not exist, and yet, according to E. Mounier's analysis, it would be generated by the absence of an "I-know-not-what": nothingness is a form of detotalization.

Our thinking on this point is diametrically opposed to his. To be sure, we recognize at the outset that nothingness does not exist. But precisely because it "is" not, its presence is incompatible with the nature of being, and it cannot take any form, not even that of detotalization. Being alone is pure positivity, i.e., capable of the act of creation that makes it being.

If we take creation as the foundation of being and as the explanatory principle of all origins; and if, on the other hand, we recognize the reality and the potency of being, then we necessarily reach the conclusion that the idea of nothingness (considered as being, non-being, or a form of detotalization) is incompatible with the notion of being, which alone is undeniable.

We do not use the term "positivity" of being in the sense of objectification, which would make being a kind of material residue, but this term enables us to single out the primary characteristic of being: self-affirmation. We thus place ourselves on a spiritual plane, higher than the objective world to which being, while human, belongs. For it is the spiritual character of being, the sign of its essence, that allows being to affirm itself as a thing-in-itself; its existence, on the other hand, ties it to the objective world, that world in which existentialist thought exclusively develops. Man, of course, relies on material means with which to define himself. But in order to know himself, he has intelligence, reason, and intuition—means of an entirely different nature. Through them man can lift himself above the world and above himself, but his constant temptation is to be satisfied with the objective realities before his eyes. They are, however, of no use to him in his true search for himself, that search which was the early ideal of the Greek thinkers.

2. The origin of the world according to St. Augustine

Here is what St. Augustine wrote about what preceded the creation of the world: "The earth was without form and void" (*inani et vacua*); "darkness was on the face of the abyss"; "light was therefore absent"; "it was like an unformed thing without any appearance" (*quaedam informitas sine ulla specie*). Let us analyze the word "abyss": the term already implies a reality, but it is used analogically, so that man can have a vague idea of the absence of being. We should at least point out that this "abyss" which preceded the creation of the universe is an outline without an imaginable appearance and without a known essence. But the end of the world will perhaps be like its beginning, when matter will be abolished. This would indicate that the word *nothingness* is there only to help us in picturing that which is not, though it means not attributing being to it. Its use is only a sign of the imperfection of human thought, which is incapable of understnding being as being. But is the word "abyss" much better?

3. *Nothingness in St. Thomas Aquinas*

Thomist philosophy gives us two troubling formulas. One comes from the neo-Thomist Maritain[1] and states that, "The creature necessarily has two origins: God and Nothingness. The other comes from Aquinas, *De Veritate* (Book II): "Things which are made of nothing tend of themselves toward nothing."

Both seem to speak of nothingness as though it had some reality, or at least as though it had its own realm. But is it not an error to look here for solution to the problem of creation? In reality, man was created in the image of God, and cannot therefore come from nothingness. Creation, of course, will never cease to be a mystery, but it is certainly tied to the creator being. If man came from nothingness, he obviously could not come from God, but, conversely, since he resembles God, he was created by Him and cannot come from nothingness. His resemblance to God is imperfect, but even if the reflection-being that is man is less perfect than the real Being that is God, man remains closer to God than to nothingness.

It is quite true, furthermore, that if man were a creation of nothingness, he would have to return to nothingness. And this would be to deny that he tends toward God. The fact that he is in the world (a world destined to be destroyed) in no way implies either that he goes toward nothingness or that he comes out of it. And it is only because the finished creature is difficult to compare with the divine Infinity that man uses the word "nothingness" to speak of himself and of his origin. We say that God created *ex nihilo* in order to give greater emphasis to the process of creation, and also to show that God did not need a distinct act of His will in order to create being. But we cannot believe in that *nihilo*, for we cannot even conceive of it intellectually, and because it is not one of those truths to which one must adhere out of faith. In our opinion, nothing would remain of the notion of man if he came out of nothingness rather than having a divine origin.

---

[1] *De Bergson à Thomas D'Aquinas*. Paris: Paul Hartmann, 1944, p. 217.

4. *Hegel's nothingness*

The best formulation of this was made by Sartre, in proclaiming the universality of nothingness as conceived by Hegel: "There is nothing in heaven and on earth that does not contain within it both being and nothingness." We need only eliminate a negative: "There is nothing in heaven and on earth that contains within it both being and nothingness." Our formula is just as clear as his, and based on stronger reasoning.

5. *Bergson's nothingness*

Bergson's concept of nothingness is of quite a different value. He explains it in *Creative Evolution*, in the chapter on "Existence and Nothingness." Bergson begins by stating that the idea of nothingness was "the invisible motor of philosophical thought" that forced man to ask himself the fundamental question from which all philosophy stems: "Why do I exist?" This doubt establishes a link between existence and nothingness. It reveals that nothingness tends to conquer being, "in order to assert itself." Thus, Bergson envisions nothingness as "a rug on which reality is stretched out," or, in other words, "like a substratum preceding being." Even if it is true, therefore, that being has always been, nothingness would exist prior to it, "at least by right, if not in fact."

Bergson uses another comparison: "However full a glass may be, the liquid filling it still fills a vacuum." Likewise, "Nothingness is filled and plugged, so to speak, by being"; and yet a third: "Fullness is an embroidery on the canvas of emptiness; being is superimposed on nothingness." But he is aware of the difference that exists between psychological or physical existence and logical existence. It is the role of metaphysics to affirm the latter, by making it a reality that can endure only by passing through nothingness. Bergson thus restores the values of duration and of free choice, placing them at the bottom of things and viewing them as the explanatory principles of their seeming mystery.

Logical existence indeed seems to arise through the sheer effect of the force immanent in truth, while physical existence needs to be explained, and would seem to be inadequate by itself to overcome nothingness. Thus, a logical principle such as A = A seems to be true for all time and to triumph over nothingness. However, a circle drawn in chalk on a blackboard has only a physical existence, and needs to be explained. But if all reality could be reduced to a mere logical existence, to an axiom or a definition, there would be no room left for efficient causality, understood in the sense of free choice. Spinoza and Leibnitz tended to adopt such an axiomatization. We prefer to follow Bergson but, aware that "2 + 2 = 4" has reality only if man is there to do the arithmetic, we reject the term "logical existence." To us, this notion is nothing other than being, the only real foundation of everything.

Likewise, rather than counterpose existence to nothingness (which reduces all reality to existence), we understand that it is being which takes the place of Bergson's nothingness, while emphasizing that there is a difference between being and existence. Moreover, to Bergson, being can be distinguished from nothingness through duration and free choice, which give being the possibility of self-affirmation. These two realities enable it to free itself from nothingness, which Bergson considers to be no more than a "pseudo-idea."

It is this pseudo-idea, however, that sparked in him the question "Why do I exist?"—a question he ultimately leaves unanswered. But also, was he not wrong to ask, "Why do I exist?" before recognizing the fact of existing? Indeed, once that point of departure is given—"I exist"—I can state by inductive reasoning: "I exist because I am; I am because I was created," thus finding that I was created because Someone was capable of creating me, which illuminates the fact of my existence. I cannot doubt that I exist, because the One who created me allowed me to know that I exist. But it is only after realizing the fact that I exist that I can dream of asking myself why.

Nevertheless, let us try to answer Bergson's question, noting that he does not try to separate it from a second question, "Why does the universe exist?" but in the first place, what does this "why" mean? It is as much a question of the goal as of the cause of existence, and the adverb certainly also takes on the meaning of "how."

Why do I exist? Because I have a role to play in the world of existence, a drama tied to the achievement of my integral being. Being human, I must give my life a human meaning.

How do I exist? Two possible meanings: first, how did I come into existence, by what process did I become human? This question poses the problem of a metaphysics of creation, which we will discuss below. Next: how am I me? I am a particular person, that is to say, I exist at a given time and in a given place; this realization leads us to what existentialism considers the central point of its philosophy: anguish. The problems of time and space underlie it. But, to us, man is not "flung into the world," in the existentialist formula, he is subject to the natural processes of birth, growth, and death. However, creation transcends matter, and man was not flung into existence like a useless object that one throws in the wastebasket! The transcendent act of his creation preceded his contact with existence, in which he can develop his innate qualities.

Thus, the question "Why do I exist?" confuses cause and goal. The cause of man's emergence lies not only in the reasons that led the Creator to create us, but in what awaits us in this world created for us. Causality and finality are but one and the same explanation of human existence: God created man for a purpose that man must discover by discovering his being, and which is, so to speak, "the cause of the cause of his creation."

Therefore, the point is not to ask why we exist; we must simply accept existence as a given. Rather than go back to the cause of our existence, we should be content to study its manifestations, such as consciousness, and we will be launched, not into "the world," but into the search for an infinite realm, the realm of creation.

Let us now take up Bergson's second question, "Why does the universe exist?" We prefer (as we said) to say that the universe was made for man rather than the reverse. The universe seems to us to be evolving toward a welcoming of man; it was necessary for the atmosphere to be transformed so that life could emerge, and the universe permits man's physical development as well as his intellectual growth. Man can nourish himself and dream in it. Man explains the Deity's plans and reveals the perfection of their accomplishment.

But man, then, realizes that he is between two infinites. The more he tries to understand the universe, which is infinitely great, the more he considers himself infinitely small. However, he understands his own greatness: endowed with a spirit, he is the image of the true Infinite. Could this be the supreme reason for the creation of the cosmos? Perhaps, in spite of everything, God created it for other purposes than man. What we know is that the universe enabled the human creature to consciously fulfill himself, and that, such as he is, he represents the most adequate form of dwelling for the being that becomes man.

In an initial reflection, Bergson admits the creative principle of the cosmos: "I connect the universe to an immanent or transcendent principle that supports it or creates it"; then, in a second stage, he seems to change his mind: "My thought rests on this principle for only a few moments." Whence this about-face? Does it not stem from a tolerance for the idea of nothingness? As far as we are concerned, we chose being in preference to nothingness, and we bow before the idea of creation, ruling out any other hypothesis. Instead of trembling, like Bergson, before the abyss of nothingness, we prefer to work backward from the creation to the creative principle, and thus to find the eternal Being. This relieves us of a new question that torments Bergson: "If a creative principle is ultimately placed at the bottom of things, the same question arises: how and why does this principle exist, rather than nothing?" For Being has its reason to be (*raison d'être*) in itself.

Thus fleeing from the principle of creation, Bergson seems to consider existence as a victory over nothingness, which leads him back to his "pseudo-idea," positing nothingness as the "substratum" of being. In reality, even in order to conquer itself, nothingness cannot precede being: being has always been. Bergson, for that matter, recognized that there is a "minus" in the picture of nothingness compared to something. But what remains of that realization, if one accepts that nothingness precedes being? What is "plus" is what precedes! Neither Bergson's duration nor free choice suffices to overcome this inferiority.

Nor is the appeal to the notion of "logical essence" a solution. For if realities of that nature appear eternal to Bergson, they are actually questionable if we agree that they are creations of the human mind. In Bergson's system, they serve to counterbalance nothingness. But if one recalls that nothingness is dust, a mere trace left by man who has gone off in search of himself, it makes more sense to get rid of this useless notion and to fully understand the idea of being.

6. From Heidegger's nothingness to the abyss

The presence of nothingness in Heidegger's system is explained by fear, that innate feeling in existential man which weakens his essential being to the point of making it receptive to the idea of nothingness. Man should not seek to discover where fear comes from, but should accept it as an inevitable fact of his existence and of the consciousness of his contingent position in the world, with respect to both his origin and his end.

Thus, in Heidegger's conception of nothingness, man driven by fear of the world wavers constantly between being and nothingness. The *Dasein* is, for a being, the fact of being in the world and being unable to abstract oneself from it. Heidegger, indeed, denies any possibility of transcendence in man: at best, he recognizes the transcendence of existence over nothingness. This quality, denied to the spirit and attributed exclusively to existence, thus remains very contingent: it is only a restrained manifestation of human freedom. It reveals a nature whose existence is tied to the world, and whose essence would be found sometimes in matter and sometimes in nothingness. So what rises before us is a being devoid of meaning, purpose, and future—a pale semblance of being, which dissolves into nothingness. Instead of using the world, which he has at his disposal in order to be more, man feels as though crushed by this mass, which he views in a disproportionate way.

This doctrine—atheist existentialism—threatens to lead to fatalism, to inaction, and by extension, to self-destruction. In this drama of the decay of the human being, the negative forces of the mind violently intervene: fear, anguish, despair gradually dissolve the individual until they obliterate him. Only the spirit, which permits a contact between the existential being and the transcendent being, can exalt man and deliver him from the crushing weight of matter.

But since nothingness is generated by fear, and since fear is a human emotion, is this not proof that nothingness is created by man?

7. The "Dasein" and nothingness

Let us recall the dual aspect of being: the existence-being and the essence-being. Let us recall that the achievement of the integral being requires the destruction of life: death marks the end of the world that lived in man, but the freed spirit can then soar above existence. The person who fell asleep on the bed of existence awakens as pure being in a state of immortality. Two formulas of Christian thinkers serve to comment on these exalting statements. One is by Claudel: "Nothingness needs only to be proclaimed by a mouth that can say: 'I am.' " The other is by G. Marcel, referring to Heidegger: "Being strangely resembles that which in his early writings he called nothingness." If being touches nothingness, it is because nothingness exists only as a function of being. Destruction goes hand in hand with existence, and, in that sense, Sartre's expression is justified: "Nothingness inhabits being." But that nothingness is not in matter, it is merely its outcome. As for the metaphysical nothingness, it does not live in us as a "thing in itself," but as an emanation of being that recalls the inexorable fate of the existent: man destroys himself; his own nature holds the seeds of his destruction. And his thought, acting in unison, creates a nothingness that destroys being.

This nothingness is generally described as an "I-know-not-what," a phantom. In his search for the foundations of being, B. Russell defined it as half-matter, half-spirit. In any event, it cannot precede matter, for that would place it in a state of potency with respect to the act, which is an outgrowth of matter-being. However, let us not forget that matter and existence are doomed to disappear and that essence must eternally triumph.

8. *Sartre's nothingness*

Sartre's *Being and Nothingness* mounts a kind of melodrama on the stage of existence. Nothingness plays the part of the villain, and the hero of the piece is being. To us, the play is absurd, since the word "nothingness" denotes the dissatisfaction that being feels with itself and with the world. But on this point, G. Marcel wrote, "By the fact that such a being maintains a living connnection to the possibility of its own nothingness...that possibility becomes what might be called an element of being." His formula is compatible with that of Sartre himself: "The being by which nothingness comes into being must be its own nothingness."

Hence, all reality, in order to be, would also need to be that which opposes it? Would it not be better that there should be nothing, rather than this kind of *danse macabre*, in which being and nothingness throw minds into confusion? They are a couple and a single thing at the same time!

This Sartrean paradox, an attempt to explain being by way of nothingness, winds up confusing the two notions so thoroughly that we no longer know which is being and which is nothingness. Reminiscences of Heidegger's thought concerning man flung into existence do not dispel the ambiguities about the relationship of being and nothingness: does man need the world in order to think? And in order to think, does he really need to "abolish" the world? It is more reasonable to say that it is the world that needs man to take on any meaning. Indeed, matter could no more be the origin of thought than the human mind could generate matter. We hold firmly to the principle of the spiritual origin of thought.

For what would be the reality of such a man, devoid of spiritual essence and reduced to a material nature? What would be his meaning, if he understands neither his relationship to the world, nor where he comes from, nor what he is?

9. *Inconsistency of Sartre's nothingness*

The essence-being is revealed through human consciousness; but while an animal, guided by its instinct, does not have to understand the environment in which it exists in order to live in this world, man grasps things around him by a process that follows consciousness of self, of which it is merely the consequence. And matter, however different it may be from spirit, draws a certain reality from that human process. Sartre, however, speaks of a nothingness immediately following being.

In face of the Hegelian formulas, he states that "being is empty of all determination other than identity with itself, but nonbeing is empty of being." He adds that however many qualities of being one takes away, one will never get it not to be. Thus, ultimately, being precedes nothingness and underlies it. However, since it draws its being from being, nothingness "haunts" being. And that is why the disappearance of being will bring about not the appearance of non-being, but rather its simultaneous disappearance. Then why not consider nothingness as a human idol that cannot be concretized? In Hegel, nonbeing fulfills the need of counterposing something to being, so that the dialectic can be applied to everything. In Sartre, it is no more than a product of being, seeking to assert and to complete itself; for being, whose original state is indeterminateness, invents (though we do not know when or how) the idol of a nonbeing, determining it by making it conscious of itself. Therefore, it is nothingness that determines being! Consciousness of self would thereby lose its immediacy, because it would depend on nonbeing.

To what end this creation of nothingness? Why imagine it in the shadow of being? If nothingness by definition is devoid of its own essence, how can it be given a being drawn from being? The notion is inconsistent, because everything in it is only a borrowing. One cannot even say that nothingness is the frontier of being, because it remains outside it. Far from asserting itself against being, it reveals its utter lack of reality.

Variations on the Theme of Nothingness

1. *Music and nothingness*

There are musical tunes that awaken in us a certain sensation of emptiness. They put consciousness into a kind of sleep, from which the opposite of a *cogito*, a kind of negative *cogito*, would emerge: "I do not think, therefore I am not." This bizarre state has neither shape nor characteristic; it is outside time, for it arises within our inner being. The emptiness to which it brings us close has some analogy with nothingness. But does it really correspond to something?

2. *Love in the face of nothingness*

Love despairs at the prospect of death, for one who loves attaches himself to the corporeal presence of the Other in the world, to the existence of the loved being. Is not such a love tantamount to slavery? The despair caused by death can produce a real vertigo of nothingness, as though this could fill the void left by the loss. With death, therefore, the temptation of nothingness can enter man's heart. The only free love is the spiritual love that attaches itself to the essence-being, and that is too deeply rooted in being to disappear with the body, leaving room for nothingness.

3. *Being, matter, and nothingness*

Nothing can either precede or follow the essence-being that we have called the "All." It therefore "abolishes" time, but we could say, on the other hand, that matter abolishes nothingness, however paradoxical that may seem. Indeed, matter is nothing without the spirit that conceives of it; after all, however, we may speak of a material nothingness opposed to matter (not to being), which therefore comes after matter. We can therefore never perceive it. It is what it will remain when the cycle of creation is finished. But we can at least consider, on the contrary, the material universe. The galaxies that arise therein do not come from a new creation to be placed on the same level as the Creation "in the beginning"; rather, they undergo a transformation in the matter which constitutes them, while the material nothingness awaits them.

The Being, on the other hand, because it will never have any relationship to any kind of nothingness, does not undergo a transformation. And Heidegger sensed that the fear of death comes from the fragility of the matter-being, which, confronted by the material nothingness, allows itself to be won over by the idea of the metaphysical nothingness. It would, of course, be better not to fear death. But how can we not fear at least the unknown quality of the beyond, so unimaginable to the material beings for which it is destined? There again, it is consciousness of our reality as essence-being that provides the solution. It helps us to come closer to our real being.

4. *Nonbeing and the universe*

The universe is expanding; it creates new spaces while the matter of the galaxies is crossing the boundaries of the unlimited at a prodigious speed. But if the physicist asks the metaphysicist, "What is there in those places that the galaxies are reaching?" the only answer that metaphysical thinking can give is "nothing." But how can this answer be reconciled with rejection of the thesis claiming that nothingness precedes matter? One would have to admit that nothingness, which appears to precede matter, is something other than nothing. In physical terms, there is no solution to the problem. But the philosopher can dimly perceive one if he tries to solve a related problem: "What was there before nothingness?" For there is a huge difference between the nothingness that preceded matter and the conceptual nothingness that "preceded" the creation of being.

But the human mind, because it is ignorant of the process of creation, uses the first notion as a symbolic image of the second. The danger is in believing that the "metaphysical nothingness" is what occupies the empty spaces toward which the galaxies are moving. How could they enter it, being physical? How to enter nothingness? Can matter coexist with it? It is, of course, unthinkable that matter could detach itself from the material realm and dissolve into nothingness. There exists, therefore, beyond the known universe, something created by God that appears infinite, but of which it is better to say that it is both indefinite and finite. Its boundaries are indefinite in relation to matter, which is incapable of reaching their end, but they are finite precisely because they pertain to matter.

Everything was different for the creation of being: before being, there was only God, its Creator.

Epilogue

1. *From nothingness to the absolute*

If we do not abandon the idea of nothingness, how will we get to the Absolute? We showed the impossibility of a coexistence between nothingness (the absence of being) and being. Any contact between nothingness and being would mean a struggle leading to their mutual destruction. What must be eliminated is the idea of nothingness, without even trying to distinguish between relative nothingness and absolute nothingness. For at bottom, man can never attain the absolute, whether it be for nothingness or for something else.

And furthermore, man could only imagine a relative nothingness if there were an absolute nothingness of which it were the image. Thus, man does not have a choice between two forms of nothingness, but between nothingness and being, death and life.

2. *Inconceivableness of nothingness*

Why is nothingness impossible, both as essence and as existence?

If everything is being, and if being is all, there is no room left for nonbeing, at least in the cosmos. Even if the human mind could devise a notion of nothingness, what purpose would that inconceivable concept serve? In speaking of "absolute nothingness," man ends by making nothingness equal to God, who alone is absolute. Man's choice lies, in reality, between God and nothingness, between God, who is everything, and nothingness, which is nothing. One might just as well call nonbeing "non-God."

3. *Unreality of nothingness and reality of the Being*

We offer two more subjects for reflection at the end of this chapter devoted to denying nothingness in the name of being:

a) Could there be an absolute nothingness instead of the infinite being?

b) Could this absolute nothingness be or exist?

In what form and with what essence?

To answer the first question, let us go back up the rungs of causality to the infinite being which is "principle in itself." Since it is the origin of everything, and since it is impossible for us to go any higher, we must conclude that it could not have been generated by a force drawn from nothingness.

To answer the second question, we state that by adopting, in spite of everything, absolute Nothingness in place of infinite Being, we run up against the worst intellectual difficulties.

What would the characteristics of nothingness be? It could not resemble either matter or spirit. Furthermore, how could something that has never existed take the place of being? On the other hand, being "is," both in the form of matter and in the form of spirit. If it were destroyed, nothing would replace it.

4. *Nothingness is emotion*

We said above that nothingness is no more than the absence of being. It is the lack caused by this absence that gives rise to the idea of nothingness in man. Furthermore, rather than "idea" it would be better to say sensation, for the lack of being is felt, and nothingness is not imagined. Just as the disappearance of a being can cause a physical sensation of absence in us, the absence of being can produce an anguish that makes us think of nothingness. The idea follows the sensation, and the consciousness of nothingness is rather on the order of psychology.

5. *Nothingness is a sign of being*

Consciousness of nothingness would, therefore, be only a poor analysis of the consciousness of being. What we call nothingness is unrecognized being.

6. *Bergson's negation*

Contrary to Heidegger, for whom negation is a universal principle, Bergson acknowledges that "negation does not create a *sui generis* idea." Nothingness would not therefore be *in se*. It is only a postulate of the human mind, seeking something to counterpose to being. In fact, nothing can oppose it, but in the anguished person, opposition between the man-being and the essence-being remains possible.

The Integral Being and the Material "Infinite" of Space

The Infinite in Us

1. The feeling of the infinite

What person does not feel an infinite within him? Yet how that infinite we feel remains impenetrable to our intelligence! It is nonetheless the essence of our spiritual life, for all life is a divine gift. Man sometimes tries in vain to stifle it in himself, but he rarely succeeds. Thus gaining consciousness of his life and essence, without ceasing to be conscious of existing, the human being has an intuition of the infinite richness of his nature.

2. The shrinking world and the grandeur of being

As human technology advances, distances shorten and space shrinks. What will the human mind, which created them, think of them? Seeing them lose their infinite aspect, will we not feel a new anguish? If we reject them, after having been ruled by them, will we not have a feeling of alienation? The best thing, of course, would be to understand how little importance they have, and to try to evade their material grip in order to rejoin the interior being. If one tries to attain the infinite, one must rise above matter, and only the spirit can accomplish this. Intelligence will never be able to do more than limit that cosmic space, the false image of the sole Infinite, the Creator.

It is only by stripping away all that is finite in him that man becomes a being. This process of "infinitization," so to speak, is what enables him to fulfill himself.

3. *The human infinite*

Man is a parcel of the infinite, however paradoxical that may appear. Since man is the resemblance of the infinite, he can and must possess the same qualities as his model, even if he is not the Infinite, even if an infinite distance lies between them.

Being and the Creation

The Creator Being

1. *Man and the "ens creatum"*

Man is both finite and infinite, because he is human and a being. Being is his essence, but man, as a human being, is plunged into existence. He is both subject to time in his existence, and immutable in his essence. But his dual destiny is in his hands: man is free. He can thus develop his being and transform himself into a being. Freedom, which is an indelible mark in him, transforms him and makes him transform the world, which he is destined to outlive as pure being.

However, in the world man builds for himself, he lives through the drama of life, for he was created with infinite possibilities, and he must, among these possible options, choose those that are an ideal for his being. He is a being in potentiality, which becomes concretized by objectifying its possibilities through action. Such is the meaning of the freedom he enjoys, of the freedom of thought that God has given him. Through them, he can to a certain degree create himself and his world, his space, his time. At the same time, however, his thought enables him to conceive of the idea of God. In searching for his being, man also encounters the real Being, the Infinite.

Why did some civilizations not develop the idea of a single, creator God? Probably because the search for being was not carried out with sufficient means, or was not completed. For in order to understand our reason to be (*raison d'être*), it is necessary to understand the mystery of creation, and we can only accomplish this by starting with man as creator of himself: the creation of man by man can then give a glimpse of the supreme creation, which it reflects. Man is both *ens creatum* and creator of himself. This seeming paradox stems from the nature of human essence, which is itself paradoxical. Existential man is indeed subject to matter; on the other hand, through his spirit, he succeeds in overcoming matter (and to a certain extent his existence). And he can also come gradually closer to his extra-existential being, which he knows as a result of divine revelation. For faith, providing a kind of intuition of the notions of spirit and of being, can supplement what the intelligence could not accomplish.

And man "sees" the creator better with the eyes of faith than he sees creation with the eyes of the body. Uncreated in time, because He is beyond time, God nevertheless has a reflection of Himself which is *ens creatum*, for there is something divine in the human soul created by Him.

2. *God's plan for man*

Man's appearance in the world was determined by an act of God's immutable will. There is a narrow link between the creator and the creation. God could not fail to create man in His image, because His will conceived him. Being also was predestined to be what it is, for the creator is necessarily creator *of* something, and because there is no creation without an object.

3. *Creator and creation according to St. Augustine*

The concept of creator does not exist without that of creation; one is complementary to the other. Thus in his *Confessions* St. Augustine asks what God did before creating the heaven and earth. Why did He not remain without doing anything? Nothing would have been created if the Creator's will had not preceded it. And if the Creator's will is everlasting, why would the creation not also be everlasting? But answers further on—that one who talks like that does not understand God. Then he poses the problem of Eternity, which he counterposes to time: for him, Eternity represents the only present, while the temporal present is only a "past pushed toward the future." That is why he clearly states that there was no "before" "preceding the creation," since "God is creator of time."

"Thy years are a day, and thy day is a today which neither gives way to tomorrow nor follows yesterday. Thy today is eternity." And St. Augustine concludes with the notion that, in truth, we can say that time exists only in tending not to be. Indeed, the past is a time which no longer is, and the future is not yet. But then, why even acknowledge the notion of time? Why refuse to see it as a product of the human imagination, an empty concept? Before the world, was there "nothing"? Was there "everything"? In reality, there was no "before," according to St. Augustine.

Creation and Being

1. *The created being as being in potentiality*

Before being created, being exists in potentiality (*in potentia*), so that the notion of "potentiality" suffices to define being (unrealized). For it is not yet anything, but it is not nothingness (for that matter, nothing is nothingness, since that concept is empty). But it is more empty than ever when it is opposed not only to being in potentiality, but to the created being, for, by its mere presence, being makes nothingness unthinkable, unthinkable even to the creative thought of God.

The notion of being in potentiality considerably clarifies the two antithetical terms, being and nothingness.

2. *Indestructibility of the Being*

Being cannot be destroyed, otherwise how would it be distinguished from nothingness? The idea of destruction is opposed to that of creation, and all of its value comes from the nondestruction of being, which is a sign of plenitude. For the grandeur of being is its "eternity": the entire creation would seem useless if it were not eternal.

But the material world and the human body are ephemeral. Only ideas, which defy the destructive power of time, survive, for they derive from being itself. They are a sign destined to make man believe that his pure being can survive death. Sartre rather seems to acknowl-

116

edge that man is entirely destructible, and the argument he gives is rather curious; he seems to say: "Man is destructible because he is a destroyer." And he contrasts the destructive action of conscious man to that of a storm, for example, which upsets the order of existing masses, but destroys nothing. Sartre assures us that man, on the contrary, knows how to destroy: and is therefore destructible.

But nothingnesss, of which Sartre believes human action capable, comes only from an apparent destruction of being. Being, in reality, survives everything.

2. *Pseudo-destruction of being*

Man could be totally destroyed only in two cases: he would perish because he had been destined to do so by the One who created him, or else he would destroy himself.

The first hypothesis is absurd: what reasons would the Creator have for putting forward the act of creation, if it would only lead to nothingness? To destroy being would be to put forward creation and its opposite simultaneously. Let us recall that for a long time the act of creation was considered as the fact of bringing a being out of nothingness, but it is more accurate to say that it is a replacement of the absence of being with being (or, better yet, with beings). For one is struck by the diversity of created beings: matter-beings, whose ephemeral properties lack the immortality proper to the spirit-being; and the spirit-being, man, who on the contrary can never be destroyed, for in him there is only a being whose essence is indestructible. In other words, his creation would lose all its value and would be reduced to a mere earthly phenomenon. We must apply in man's case the contradiction that would be inherent in a creation subject to destruction.

Let us therefore exclude the first hypothesis and turn to the second, stating that man, because he did not create himself and can only make himself more and more complete, cannot destroy himself either. G. Marcel, analyzing Sartre, compares Sartrean man to "a miniature God," without, however, acknowledging his power to destroy himself. His mortality is just the opposite of the power of self-destruction: it is suffered, so that man can be for himself neither a creative deity nor a destructive deity.

Creation and Nothingness

1. The act of creation in the face of nothingness

Before examining the creative act in relation to nothingness, we must repeat here that the mere affirmation of being implies the absolute negation of nothingness, even as a form opposed to being. And we must reject the sophisms that create nothingness in order to counterpose it to being, as though that opposition helped being to assert itself. Being can do without that kind of help or any other: it draws its foundation, its substratum, from creation.

But what is creation? It is only by analogy that we call it an act, for act implies action and the realm of "doing" is strictly human. Creation is an intrinsic quality, closely tied to being. One cannot imagine it without being, or being without it. What we see throughout creation is God Himself, in the manifestation of His infinite grandeur; but it should be clear that neither the term "manifestation" nor "act" is precisely suitable. Something remains in all of this that transcends our intelligence, and that is the very mystery of being.

Once created, man lives, thinks, exists. But existence is conceivable only as subordinate to creation. It is only the result of the union of each being's own essence with consciousness, thought, and life.

Creation takes place independently of time; it takes place within being itself, with all the potentiality it gives it. But then, how can God be, if He was not created? There again is a question that surpasses human intelligence, at least as much as the mystery of creation. The answer is that with man's fall, his intelligence lost its fundamental capacities, particularly that of immediacy: these capacities can no longer be used on intermediate objects. Neither creation nor the nature of God are immediately comprehensible to man any longer. Human thought vainly strives to place itself on a level with God, who is both the riddle and the solution to these questions.

Since we are ignorant of the principles, let us begin our argument at the end, even at the risk of upsetting the logical order: for that matter, it is not all that illogical to confuse the principle and the goal in God. And the idea of God can clarify our thoughts about our being: beginning with God, we arrive at man, just as one may arrive at God by beginning with man.

Having stated as much, can we make a similar argument for going from matter to man? Will the problem of the creation of matter, if it is rationally intelligble to man, enable him to solve his own problem? What is creation, then? What is matter? The next two chapters will try to answer these questions.

Creation and Matter

1. Creation, universe, and nothingness

The creation of the universe is portrayed in the Bible with great evocative power. The cosmos is born from the *fiat lux*. But if we accept that there was a beginning, logic decrees that there must also be an end. Should we try to reconcile the story of creation with the theories of modern physics?

According to these theories, galaxies are constantly being formed in an expanding "universe." This would imply re-creations, which are difficult to reconcile with the idea of a single creation, followed by the Creator's "rest." In reality, the births of these galaxies are due to a transformation of matter, rather than to new creations. Here also, the calculations of Sir Arthur Eddington and of James Jean on the rate of expansion of stellar matter should be recalled.

An extraordinary event would have occurred 5 or 10 billion years ago;* this statement fits in rather well with the old Biblical account. Furthermore, Smith's machine has calculated our current distance

---

* The original version of this book was written between September 1955 and February 1957, when the "age" of the known universe had not yet been estimated, as it has now, at up to 20 billion years. This was recently confirmed when light from quasars was intercepted after a long trip of some 18 billion years.

from the remotest galaxies: nearly 2 billion light years. These two figures are on the same order of magnitude, and we can imagine that accumulations of mattter were launched into the universe at the time when *fiat lux* occurred; but we will have to wait a few billion years for proof of their accuracy by which time our sun may already have disappeared from the universe!

At what point in the world and with what matter did God create the cosmos? Did He create it out of nothingness? At most, it would be a material nothingness, impossible for man to imagine, but nonetheless different from the metaphysical nothingness, which is an absurdity. Nothing could logically have existed prior to the *fiat lux*. As St. Augustine explains, the notion of time loses all usefulness when it is a question of explaining creation, for time itself was created by God in the same creative act as the world.

There is an essential relationship between creation and the universe. And there can be no question of a re-creation, given the extratemporal unity of the creative act.

Epilogue

1. *The initial impulse—enigma of the creation*

God gave an initial impulse to matter. He created the universe with a whole potentiality for expansion. At the beginning, everything was perhaps reduced to molecules or atoms. But because of this potentiality, what had been a "semi-nothingness" took on the dimensions of an immense reality. The cosmos was created and endowed with motion and expansive force, and while astronomers have taken it upon themselves to calculate the date of its creation, no one has yet dared to say when matter will lose all of its momentum.

Motion is not a law, but a destiny to which matter is subject: the galaxies that are half a million light years away are zooming at 160 kilometers per second; those that are 250 million light years away reach a speed of 40,000 kilometers per second, and those that are a billion light years away reach 75,000 kilometers per second. In other words, the farther they are from the beginning, the greater is their speed; it increases with distance.

. There is no law of this kind in human destiny. Rather, man has been given the privilege to be free and to disobey all natural laws; while these laws control his existence, he dominates them as pure being. His body, no doubt, will return to dust, but eternity is in his

122

essence. What does it matter, then, if a parallel is made between the destiny of man's body and that of the cosmos—both traveling toward a death that resembles nothingness—if man, as spirit-man, without needing either re-creation or reappearance, is capable of conquering death?

It is the cosmos, which despite its immensity cannot escape the fatal law, that may be considered a "piece torn from infinity."

2. *The paradox of paradoxes*

The quantum theory has a philosophical dimension. We are amazed to learn that each atom is made up almost entirely of emptiness; matter is practically "immaterial." However, it is also made up of perpetual motion. According to Bertrand Russell, this theory would explain the world in a more satisfactory way than Einstein's famous relativity theory. Russell, after Eddington, remarks that "the world is becoming increasingly disorderly"; it might be blocked if its elements were not put back in order. For his part, Sir Arthur believes that "despite evolution, which introduces a growing organization in the earthly sector of the universe, there is, in general, a gradual disorganization, which, in the long run, will annul all the organization due to evolution.... The entire universe will reach a stage of complete disorganization, which will be the end of the world." Thus, atoms are not completely subject to determinism, and the law of causality is challenged at the level of the universe. The author concludes that scientific analysis steeps the world in unreality and irrationality, and that order, unity, and continuity are human inventions.

If it is indeed true that matter is made up of electrons whose motion is independent of any mechanical law, it would be astonishing that such a degree of unpredictability should be compatible with any form of physical determinism. And yet this disorder creates a majestic order in heaven. The entire universe seems to perfectly execute the Creator's plan. That "clock" which impressed Voltaire obeys a supreme will, which we call "order" or "disorder" in the tiny degree to which we can interpret it.

Negation of Time in the Name of Being; Rhythm and Time

Analysis of Time

1. *In the abyss of time*

Before the abyss of time, as before infinite space, man feels tiny and lost. But in reality, it is his own thought which has created those two "infinites," unfortunately defining them poorly, however, so that it is their share of the unknown that both frightens and appeals to man. His intelligence drives man to explore space and time, but faith leads him to transcend them. In this experiential drama, the human being fulfills himself by seeking to know himself at all costs, and he uses the means God has given him to liberate and to assert himself: consciousness, reason, will, freedom. Of course, consciousness of his existence comes in the context of time and space, but it also helps him to transcend those facts by giving him the intuition that he "is."

Planck criticized the materialist utopia, pointing out that matter is indeterminateness, since no one can say with accuracy where a given electron is at a given moment. Furthermore, determinism seems to be absent from the physical laws that attempt to explain matter. Let us try to distinguish determinism from finalism, for a certain purposefulness might actually guide that indeterminateness; electrons, atoms, and molecules seem to move toward the same goal, and biology likewise provides examples of finalism, implying an "intelligent" course on nature's part.

But man is a being apart: he is free and conscious. Only his consciousness can guide him through time and space. Heidegger, in *Being and Time*, tried to reduce consciousness to the consciousness of existing. But the "existing" should rather be called "being," because being *is* its existence and moreover must realize itself as being. It "is" in time, because it lives its present as a function of its past and future; but for those very reasons, it is always more. Thanks to his being, man rises above time, of which he was the creator, somewhat as God was his, but which he is destined to destroy, whereas God will not destroy being. So as not to lose his bearings in existence, man created time, but it is a myth as ephemeral as those of the old mythologies.

2. *Subjective time*

What is the essence of time? Nothing. It passes differently according to the moment; at night, dreams of a few seconds seem to last for hours.

It is even less tangible and more unreal than space. Both are reflections of the outside world on consciousness, and when consciousness is cut off from the world (during fainting, for example), they are both distorted. It is clear that the reason they have no life of their own apart from consciousness is that they are subjective.

Moreover, time does not have the same meaning for everyone. What are sixty years to a mountain? If, then, time is one thing to A, another thing to B, yet another thing to C, and to D nothing at all, is it not a useless measurement?

3. *Time as a notion*

Man creates time to better understand the succession of human events to give them a cohesiveness that can maintain the unity of the driving force. He uses it as a gradual curve, and if we can say that he rises with this curve, it is not, in any case, what gives him the energy necessary for his climb.

Let us argue from the absurd and imagine a life without time: it is livable. Certain experiments have proved this: one may survive without a temporal framework, it is not a prerequisite for the human being. Being is indeed indestructible, and it transcends space and time, whatever they are. For the "motion-time" of Heraclitus is no more valid than the "spatialized" time of the physicists; combining the notions of time, distance, and motion makes the three elements even more insubstantial. One could not speak of time in itself, for there is no time-being.

Time and space are on the same order of reality as cause and effect; they are distant consequences of general principles. All of these concepts are used by man to understand the universe, which order, however, is nontemporal and immutable, having been created by God who is infinite. In any case, time, which is relative to each individual and has no being of its own, is neither a negation nor an affirmation. If it were a negation, it would be as empty as the concept of nothingness; if it were an affirmation, it would exist outside individual consciousnesses, instead of varying according to each one.

One may, of course, object that time is based on the succession of days and nights, and that the sunrise is located outside of psychological consciousness. That is true, but is it not clear that by obliging man to regulate his life and intelligence by astronomical data, one would make time into a God? But God—who gave the world a chronology— also created eternity, and there is no celestial body which can help man to imagine it.

To revere time as man's conqueror is to forget that living beings age according to a natural order that is independent of time. Time has no destructive power in itself, it is only the "accompanying wave" of human destiny, which has been limited by sin. To see a cause and effect relationship between time and death is false reasoning, for in fact, each person's life and the history of nations depend solely on God.

4. *Time as "smoke"*

Time has no reality, it is not a being. It may be compared to the smoke emitted by being, if being is defined as a flame. And we know that smoke takes away fire's light and heat. Thus, time makes us think of death; it is responsible for many moral errors and for many struggles. But conversely, we may say that if there were no death, man would not have thought of inventing a time line with which to measure his life. By trying always to lengthen that line, he becomes obsessed by instants as by pieces of gold. And the past, for him, is a kind of treasure—the past only, for the present does not exist and the future is not yet. But one cannot even say that the past is, for it no longer is, and time, therefore, is something neither to acquire nor to lose.

For that matter, it is not time which passes, it is us. We burn ourselves up at the sometimes senseless pace which it imposes. But it is this very drama which, by making our life more intense, can make it lovelier, whereas the inactive contemplation of time may, on the other hand, cause anguish. Time must become rhythm in order to become life for the being-man.

Rhythm and Time

Motion is one of the most visible phenomena in the universe. It exists in many forms: transformation, displacement, the passage of time, etc. And we can barely distinguish time from the flow of events for which it serves as a reference point. But if we refuse to use this conventional notion of time, what can we discern in the mass of the world? How can we understand, one by one, the things of life? In other words, is it still possible to perceive and to think without time? Let us say at least that there is a certain rhythm that lies behind all the elements of creation, life, and beings.

But that rhythm is not time itself; it corresponds to a deeper notion that partakes of being and of essence. Thus, even if we can dispense with time, we cannot imagine the world having been created without the idea of a rhythm. Every thing has its rhythm, and motion is thus expressed naturally in it, that is, according to the will of the Creator. It is He who gave Creation its initial impetus, as well as the rhythm by which it develops.

Time is a measurement, and it remains in the quantitative realm, but rhythm is qualitative and therefore immeasurable. We must desist from explaining the world in terms of time and give rhythm its rightful place—rhythm, inherent in being, which alone will rebuild what time threatens to destroy. For what must reign over the entire universe is essentially a harmony.

2. *Vital force of rhythm*

What is a force? Is it not a cause that we judge by its effects? Bertrand Russell, in discussing astronomy, denies the existence of "forces"; rather, he believes in a correlation between sidereal bodies. He takes the example of a mirror and compares the motion of planets to that of reflected images. No force impels those images, and yet they move. Cannot a similar argument be made concerning human history? Are not historic causes and their effects fictitious explanations, corresponding to no reality in this world? For Bergson, to divide life into its different elements is tantamount to killing living beings, which are complex: the notion of cause and effect, applied to humanity's history, would break up its vital unity. It would be better to admit that a complex rhythm determines human destiny, without, however destroying freedom.

To be sure, man appears enslaved to his destiny as a mortal, but he remains free to choose his life's ideal, and his actions flow from the decisions made by his will.

3. *Vital rhythm and the human being*

Time is a measurement of life's passing. Rhythm, on the other hand, is a manifestation of life that creates itself.

In short, time contributes nothing: rhythm creates everything. Time is merely a fictitious notion, while rhythm is a reality that is felt. Each life moves toward a beyond, but can reach it only by keeping up the rhythm of the creative force. Enslaved by time, man could only march toward death, whereas rhythm keeps him free for uninterrupted progress. We saw that time—which, for example, is different for man than for a mountain—prevents creatures from living in unison. Rhythm, however, being the manifestation of all life forms, makes possible true harmony among the different elements of the universe.

4. *Time and motion*

The notion of time is linked to that of motion, Aristotle taught. The unending flow of all things astonished him. But how much more astounded he would be by modern physics! He never heard, for example, of the speed of light, the very thing that compelled Einstein to invent a fourth dimension—space-time.

5. *Slowing of rhythm*

We can understand life better when we speak of its rhythm rather than of its time. The notion of time takes on an enormous psychological importance near the end of a human life, when the years are "counted." On the other hand, one's vital rhythm slows down quite naturally when one's vitality diminishes; it slows down, then stops in relation to life. Is that not a proof of the close relationship that rhythm maintains to the essence of beings?

6. *Rhythm of lives and duration of beings*

"Each plant originates with a cell, which does not contain the product that must emerge from it, but which possesses, or at least is accompanied by, a force which causes and controls all of its future development."[1] This statement by Alphonse de Decandolle forces us to ask a question about the development of beings: are they subject to the destructive force of time, or rather to a vital force such as Bergson envisions? On the other hand, time and duration must not be confused; in the course of time, beings are transformed, whereas duration insures the internal unity of each being.

The notion of duration is necessary to man, who through it recognizes himself, but he can dispense with "time" in order to understand himself and the world.

7. *Rhythm is life; life is rhythm*

Human life knows two kinds of rhythms, one physical and vital, the other spiritual and mental. Man perceives one in his body and the other in his spirit. But only consciousness can perceive the rhythm of being, which is both motion and eternity.

---

[1] Alfred Russel Wallace: *El Mundo de la Vida*, Madrid: Daniel Jorro, editor, p. iii (Preface).

Time and Being

1. *Immutability of being and the notion of time*

Although man is transformed, his being endures: in the course of existence, his essence can perfect itself and become ever more itself, but it remains substantially immutable, otherwise being would cease to be being.

G. Marcel criticizes Bergson's idea of time as an uninterrupted series, which would not allow the being to really be. Thus he writes: "As a mere spectator, supposing myself to be in a state of extreme fatigue or perhaps merely of perfect relaxation, I let them flow past me, as, on the edge of a stream one lets the current flow past." But he adds: "But in so far as there is a real substance in my life, or in anybody's life, it is impossible that my life should reduce itself to a mere flow of images, and impossible therefore that its structure should be merely that of a succession."[1] Moreover there can be a succession only for a consciousness which transcends it. The abstract is, indeed, resistent to any succession.

But if Bergson placed perhaps too much importance on the series, he at least deserves credit for conceiving of life as being one and indivisible, thus giving it a certain degree of substantiality. Unfortu-

---

[1] *The Mystery of Being, Vol. I: Reflection and Mystery.* Chicago: Henry Regnery Company, 1970, p. 233.

nately, it is difficult to separate the two realms of unity and of a series. If it is important that experience be continuous, since its stages form a whole and thus a substance, how to reconcile this substance with time which destroys it, and say whether being is a series as existence, or a unity, as essence? We should at least point out that abstract being is not subject to the passage of time, like matter and concrete being. Rather, it follows the rhythm of life, when it has taken the shape of a human personage. But this interdependence between the unfolding of life in man and the substratum of being awakens in us a fertile metaphysical curiosity.

Let us now consider the possible transformations of being in time: man belongs to the world of matter through his body, but he is also capable of elevating his spirit and of affirming himself as a transcendent being. He can, just as freely, reach toward baseness or toward grandeur. Now, the living cells of the human body are renewed over the years, but the system's physiological functioning does not change. This is so because it is not living matter which is the essence of the human body, but its unity: the life of the body develops at a rhythm that is characteristic of it. If the cells are renewed in an identical way, it is because of a unity-generating force completely independent of time. But since man has difficulty understanding his nature, he often believes it is a question of fleeting time, and he bemoans the fact that he cannot hold it back.

The question remains, why does the vital rhythm lead being from life to death, and why is there death?

2. *Time as a human notion*

We do not agree with Bergson that time is an uninterrupted series of events, because, for us, it is nothing of the kind: it is a fictitious convention, an empty notion, which man uses the better to organize his life, but which has no concretization in reality. At best, it provides a few reference points that enable memory to organize chaotic perceptions; but this concept must be demystified, this false god must be desecrated. Above all, we must remember that the real God created His work without time. The creation was designed for eternity, which rules out any interference by time.

Moreover, it is only in civilized societies that man, like Gulliver, gives the impression of worshipping his watch. In all places where the vital force is more in evidence, time seems neither to rule the world nor to lead it toward a goal. At best, it gives man the past, and the future is felt to belong to God alone. Time appears as a guardian of the archives of our past history, as pure subjectivity to which it is useless to make appeals.

3. *Existence and nostalgia*

Within the integral being, we distinguished the principle-being and the existence-being. Time is essentially of the same nature as the latter, since it is a human intuition of emotional origin. Man fears death as the end of existence in the world; however, death aids him in attainment of the principle-being, for man, through death, fulfills himself in true richness, beyond the existential adventure of his destiny. With this prospect in view, man should replace his anguish with hope, and there have even been wise men and saints who wished for death.

We now envision, not being in relation to the end of its earthly existence, but all men in relation to death, which will lead us back to Heidegger, for the latter's notions of nothingness are based on fear. In reality, nothingness is one of the possible images of death. Anguish, nothingness, and death are thus confused in the human psyche, which is imprisoned by these spatial-temporal categories. To overcome his anguish, man would have to reject the images of time, the only function of which is to remind him of the inexorable limit placed on his earthly life. Let him think of death as something other than an end. What importance will time have then?

If man is able to control his reactions as an existence-being and to despise death, he will attain the integral being, which is immortal. That certainty should dispel his anguish over the future, as well as his nostalgia for the past.

Einsteinian Time and Augustinian Time

1. *Einstein and relativity*

Einstein reduces the notions of time and space to the gravitational force of matter, for without a material mass, there would be neither radiation nor energy. And he merges space with time in a fourth dimension, enabling each system to have its own time, which, thus spatialized, becomes material. It is therefore more a physical deduction than a reality in itself, but nonetheless will have an end, necessarily conditioned by the disappearance of matter.

This matter is in constant transformation, that is a recognized fact. But Einstein sees this transformation, in reality, as a race toward disintegration, the universe being gradually dissolved in a void so perfect that the human spirit cannot imagine it. Before giving our opinion on this rather despairing vision, let us quote Lincoln Barnett[1]: "In a few billion years, all the processes of nature will have to stop: all of space will have the same temperature, and it will be impossible to use energy, because it will be uniformly distributed throughout space. There will be neither light, heat, nor life. All will be perpetual and irrevocable stagnation. Time itself will come to an end.... There is no way of avoiding this fate, for the second law of thermodynamics declares that the fundamental processes of nature are irreversible."

---

[1] *6 Universos o Dr. Einstein*. São Paulo: Companhia Melhoramentos, p. 94.

But later, the same author corrects himself: "In light of the Einstein-ian principle of the equivalence of mass and energy, it is possible to imagine that the radiation dispersed in space should again condense into particles of matter, which combine to form bigger units, and thus the vital cycle of the universe can repeat itself to eternity and beyond."

But since different calculations, on the other hand (the accelerating speed of the galaxies, for example), have led to the conclusion that something had to exist beforehand (universal substance, cosmic essence), we can recognize that there is an ever-present rhythm which everything obeys. This rhythm, in our view, is the expression of a divine will.

To accept the hypothesis of a perpetual re-creation of the universe would be to admit that neither the cosmos nor "time" will have an end. Time, in that case, is no different from eternity. On the other hand, if matter is moving toward inexorable destruction, it becomes impossible to conceptualize time as a being-in-itself, conceivable at the scale of the entire universe. For if, as Einstein calculates, the cosmos equals 200 billion light years, this means that time exists only within a system, and that it cannot be applied to the entire cosmos.

Thus reduced to the scale of a system, instead of being deified, as it was by ancient man, what does time become? A being in itself? A being subject to the universal law? A rhythm of life? Let us say rather an accompaniment to the rhythm of life, that lucid but inexorable condition which is imposed on all existence by the will of the Creator.

Would this law apply also to the integral being in eternity, as it does for the existential being? We cannot accept this, for the being is subject to no rhythm once it has found its immutable eternity.

2. The Augustinian conception of time

When St. Augustine asks this question—"What did God do before creating the heaven and earth?"—it must be emphasized that he used the past tense of the verb. But how could God act within time, since time has no relationship to creation? God is the act: everything He does, He does in the present, a present that for Him has neither change, interval, nor succession. Only the thing created can change, and not through the action of time, but through its power to develop at its own rhythm. It is God who determines that rhythm for each of His creatures, while remaining above it.

But St. Augustine further says, "There is no time in which Thou hast done nothing, for time is Thy work." We think that if God created time, it was through the intermediary of the human brain, by giving it the power to think, to conceptualize, and to imagine.

For St. Augustine, time "exists while tending not to be." But for us, that which tends not to be is nothing, exactly like that which is not, but tends to be. Being is, or it is not; but if it "is," it "is" immediately.

This, time "is" not, because it tends not to be, unlike the human being, who, being spiritual, tends always to be more, because he tends toward God.

Let us go back to the Augustinian formula. If God did nothing before time, He did nothing afterward either, for otherwise He would be subject to that "time" which, tending not to be, could not be considered as a *sine qua non* of creation; and creation would cease to be a pure act. Moreover, if God did nothing before time, we may wonder how He could then have created it, for time alone produces motion and action, and one imagines in God a state of paralysis which He would have had to end in order to begin the act of creation! What would remain of our concept of an infinite and eternal God, who is perfect and thus immutable? It is therefore not God who created it (we have already stated that it was man; let us add this time that he wasted his time in doing so).

Since human nature is contingent, it fell back on time to explain its contingency to itself, and if, in this sense, time can apply to man, it can never apply to God. For that matter, man makes his own history and lives by his own forces. The universe and man are "torn pieces of infinity" and are destined for a perfection located outside of spatial-temporal concepts.

St. Augustine also makes this argument: if, in order to create, it was necessary that a new will should arise within God, the Creator would not be eternal; God's will precedes creation, for otherwise no being could have been created. But God's will brings forth a perpetual creation; God would contradict Himself if the being in potentiality and the created being were not exactly symmetrical. Creation and creature are combined in a state that is likewise extratemporal. Man has always been part of the divine plan of creation, and a plan conceived by the Infinite can admit no alteration. Thus, the human being was predestined to be, and he is.

The problem of time, as posed by St. Augustine, has a broad metaphysical scope: time could not exist before God created it, and since God creates independently of time, time is not a divine creation.

Time and Matter

1. *Time and the universe*

The more the rhythm of life is imposed on the universe, the more the importance of time decreases: it could never, for example, serve to measure human emotions. Likewise, it is insufficient as a scale for the infinite mass of galaxies that make up the universe, so prodigious is their rhythm; the distances that separate them from man are such that the measuring instrument that man has devised seems absurd.

The notions of time and of the universe are antagonistic. It is necessary to say that time is too small or that the universe is too large. In order to understand the universe, it will be necessary to devise concepts other than those of time and space.

2. *Divisibility of time, space, and matter*

Is it rationally possible to divide time, space, and matter *ad infinitum*?

Divisibility to infinity is in itself a sign of infiniteness. Is this true of time? How can we accept this? As for matter, we know from the progress of physics that it is in fact immaterial: invisible forces stamp

139

it with the motion of life. We can agree that it is "practically nothing," hardly more than time. We would therefore have little difficulty in "abolishing" it. Finally, space can be conceived of only in relationship to matter, and is therefore nothing in itself. It is not divisible to infinity, for its proportions are not infinite, but are limited to those of matter. The space traveled by certain particles in a millionth and even a billionth of a second ceases, for all practical purposes, to be locatable. Such spaces are so small that these particles can be considered as extratemporal. They arise without any necessity because they belong to a world different from that which the human mind tries to imagine. These, therefore, are the obvious conclusions: time and space are nothing but pure mental images without foundation in reality and without existence. Matter exists. Being is. Space and time appear, at best.

3. *Time is matter*

Are space and time physical properties of matter, as yet unknown? In any case, they would be linked to the idea of motion, and if matter should cease to move, would they not automatically disappear?

Even if one assumes that time is matter, it is rhythm that is life.

Time and Eternity

1. *God and time*

For God and in God, everything is immediate: potentiality and becoming do not exist. His will is concretized or fulfilled immediately. The being which at first is in potentiality, then comes into the world and disappears from it, is seen by Him as separate from the image of time, for God is infinite Presence. If everything that God does, He does immediately, God has no need of time; otherwise, we would have to admit that time is infinite. A subservience to the future would imply the non-divinity of God, because He would be subject to improvement. And if He is pure perfection, how can perfection and time be united? Time is the image of extension for the being that develops itself.

God lives neither in time nor in space, because space could not contain Him and time would limit Him.

2. *Death and eternity*

Will man, after life, lose consciousness of his being, which, on earth, is rather closely tied to his spirit, so much so that it is nearly confused with his being, because there is no boundary between consciousness of self and being. The being which become man has the conscious certainty of being a being. Will we be forced to admit that after life, we would lose the notions of space, time, existence, as well as the being which we are? Is man nothing more than an animal with a universal vocation?

If we do not transform into anything, will we be transformed into nothingness? Can nothingness be something which persists across time? If man and the universe are reduced to nothingness, nothingness must probably have preceded them, must have existed prior to being, and prior to everything! But if nothingness had existed prior to things and to being, we would be nothing, we would not even be able to be, nothing would be. But just as chaos does not precede order, nothingness likewise did not exist prior to being, or else there would be neither being nor order nor any reason for things and for everything to be. If something exists, a Being exists prior to man and to the Universe by His will: it is outside time and resists its destructive power.

How can we believe that man, things, the universe would be created and later swallowed up by nothingness? How can we believe in a man stripped of meaning, a being without purposefulness, a creation without a goal, matter without life? The goal exists as a function of the principle, and that goal is immortality.

3. *Time before God*

What is time for God? It is barely a horizon for man! It brings the succession of human events and the unfolding of things: the former are unpredictable, while the latter are subject to a certain determinism imposed in general by a divine hand—the growth of a plant, the trajectory of a planet or a star.

This succession of events gives man the impression of time. But this impression remains cerebral, it does not create a reality, neither in itself nor in the eyes of God; it is valuable only in relation to things and to man, author of these unpredictable events. Was Heidegger not correct in defining times as a "horizon of *Dasein*" and in believing that it counts for much less in the divine creation than light, energy, and matter!

4. *Eternity of life*

Bergson labeled eternity "the eternity of life"; he could not imagine anything that was not endless motion and succession. He seems to have foreseen the atomic world we know today; he plunged into the objective world, strongly reflecting the influence of Spencer. But his "eternity of life" does not exist, in spite of the meaning he tried to give the expression, for life implies motion, time, rhythm, and succession, and eternity transcends all of this, everything that man knows, everything that exists in the world. It even rises above the spirit, which is immortalized by death, because eternity is God, and God alone can enjoy it. It "is" only as a function of the Creator. And the Creator did not create it, for it emerged spontaneously from Him.

If, on the one hand, there are no moments in eternity, because God is above time, we must not forget to point out that stagnation does not exist either, for there is nothing in it which resembles the things of the world and of man. Man is capable of understanding everything that surrounds him, but nothing in his spirit is made to give him an image of eternity, so that nothing in eternity is made to be understood by man—neither time nor motion nor paralysis. It is purely a question of atmosphere, infinitely distant from the material being. And we cannot visualize a "place," within us or outside of us, in which to locate eternity.

For humans, it can only be nothing: not in a negative sense, of absence of being or of the being's flight toward the void, but as something that the human brain cannot imagine. To the contrary, it will be everything for the essence-being, the being that is wholly spiritualized at the moment of its death.

5. *Time, "continuation of eternity"*

If, in reality, there exists no communion between subject and object, if we do not know how they come in contact, if human intelligence cannot penetrate to the essence of matter, how can we try to consider time as the continuation of heavenly time, that is, of eternity?

If eternity is an absurdity for our poor human understanding, what an even greater absurdity time would be, if it were something!

6. *Time and death, or the death of time*

For St. Augustine, time consists of the past, present, and future, but, in addition, there is the pressure of the past on the future, and the destructive power of the future on the past. Time is a struggle which never ends, because of the constant re-creation of new moments.

Time is less complicated: it does not attack being. It is purely human, because it is a human creation. Its foundation is the fear of death, which dominates the idea of the future. Man feels attached to the present, and he needs to cling to it, without ceasing to look backward. Since death will inevitably come to man, he invented time, in order to protect the ashes of the past in his internal temple, and to try to become master of the rhythm of his life.

7. *Machines for "going back in time"*

Ideas of time across the centuries are varied and contradictory. The disintegration of time, due to the Einsteinian physics of relativity, leave us a kind of regret for that shadow which, for so many centuries, accompanied humanity, as if to protect it against the hostility of the cosmos, against the assaults of universal matter.

Time flies and does not get tired ("Time flows steadily on," said James Jeans), because time is linked to life. And it makes us believe that it is time which flies, when in reality, it is life, the peculiar rhythm of each life, which goes forward without stopping. If there were no motion in objective reality, man would not have created the notion of time. And if, outside the world, there is no motion, if everything there is silence and the abode of pure being, there is no need of time.

But man, so long as he is human, will not alter the incessant rhythm of life. His history will not retrace itself, because it is moved by inexorable laws, as powerful as the laws of decay which govern the world's matter. That backward march of time of which men often dream could be lived only by a pure being, a disembodied spirit. But when the flesh is resurrected, spirits will once again be in "time," because they will again enter into life and will be reincarnated: that is the only backward march of time which can be imagined, that return to a life whose rhythm has already stopped.

For one who abandons the world and penetrates the regions of the unknown loses the notion of time—for him, all is present, and there is no waiting. What pure spirits will feel is a return to life and to existence, similar to the return of memories that come back to us in thought. But what sensation do we have when we think back on our past life? That of going back in time? No, we return to the past, reliving the forgotten emotions of those times, but without the notion of time.

If time is the rhythm of life, it is pure emotion and essentially human; it is a sign of life.

8. *Time, the creation of matter*

There exists a physical time, a chronology which is quite different from deified time, the destroyer of man. Stars and light create time by their trajectories through space. That is why Aristotle based time on motion. But in fact, modern physics interprets the universe in non-material terms; it has discovered that it is not matter. It is therefore a true contradiction to materialize time. If nothing moved in the cosmos, what would it be?

But if space is nothing, and if motion is produced, not across the emptiness which bears that name, but across matter which makes up all bodies; if, finally, that motion comes only from the expansion proper to each body and to matter in general, how can we conceive of time? Is it not a creation of matter?

9. *A glance at eternity*

Man becomes anxious when he tells himself that, after his death, his soul will live forever; it is because be cannot stand so much light, and because he still has the desire for time, a necessarily unsatisfied desire, for time is based on earthly life, it is the desire to live.

The shores of the unknown exert a pull on man who is living his life, who is eager to live ever longer, and to feel the emotion of running: by running, he lives. But at the same time, he needs a past, and he knows in spite of everything that the future, in the last analysis, represents his end.

But these are all things of the world, all of this is the world. Outside the world there is only spirit. And in the realm of the spirit, eternity (or better, immortality), all is reality; the anguish of time cannot be felt there, for it is the fear of death. That is why it is good that from time to time man should come out of himself and cast a quick glance at eternity.

Negation of Space in the Name of Being

Notions of Essence

1. The absence of matter

Space in relation to matter is a little like what nothingness represents for being. Space is the absence of matter, but not an absolute absence, for matter would cease to be a reality if it could be reduced to nothingness at one point. Where there is no visible matter, space gives the impression of encompassing everything, and man considers it as a being, giving it particular characteristics. Now, space is extension, and that very fact makes it difficult for man to know what it really is. As being, it must have limits, and as matter, it must have a beginning and an end, shape, color, properties. But since man can neither limit it nor know it boundaries, how can we make it a material being? It unfolds before us, it has the apparent characteristics of matter, it is one step away from us, since we are encompassed by it, and yet it has not been duly defined.

It is true that space makes matter's motion possible. How could a star follow its course without it? And yet, it is not a being, it merely concedes to matter the power to be what it is, to grow, to move.

But it is the conditions under which matter moves which compel man to have an idea of space. Space did not exist prior to matter; it did not emerge first so that matter would occupy it; it is the apparent equidistance of one body to another, or, in a single body, of one molecule to another, without representing something in itself.

This definition shows a similarity between space and nothingness, which is nonbeing or absence of being, because everything which exists is material. However, in the mind of homo sapiens, this concept is useful for imagining matter: as matter advances, making something of what was nothing, generating new universes, as it emerges and appears, it forms around it what we call space, but which is more convention than reality. For the stars and constellations change position for man, who finds a point of reference determining their displacement, but space is not a being independent of matter; it is matter, although of immaterial appearance.

The defenders of the notion of space do not see matter everywhere, and conclude that the universe is made up both of matter and of space. It is rather made up of emptiness and of bodies, and if we could unite in a single block all the matter of the cosmos, how small it would become! But that is an absurd idea: the cosmos can never be condensed, for it is not a question of space, but of the arrangement of matter. Matter, at its creation, was arranged in the manner which still characterizes it. The distances from body to body, from molecule to molecule, from atom to atom, from electron to electron, will never change, and are comparable to those separating the sidereal bodies. So that space does not constitute a reality; it is at least a factor of celestial harmony. Esthetics, poetry, lyricism, and beauty become its reason to be.

It appears to human eyes as the ether where the planets conduct their gigantic march. But even Einstein gave up trying to define the world ether, and no one knows what it is. Neither space nor ether possess conditions of existence, and they do not exist as beings in themselves in the universe. They are nice abstractions which man invents in his dream of better understanding how the stars move about up there. For how could the stars move if the infinite were full of something corporeal? It seems quite evident that all motion demands that there be no solid matter in its path. To this purely logical absence of matter, the name space was given.

But contemporary physics has discovered that the universe is "curved," and above all, that it has an end. But, though having an end, it does not have limits, because it is limited by space, which is nothing. Thus, one can also call it unlimited, but one cannot call it the infinite. As though it were possible to chain the infinite to dead matter! The universe will cease when the motions that transport it toward the beyond, toward the unknown, cease and it will surely never reach its limits, which do not exist.

2. *The idea of the infinite*

The human conception of the infinite is of a strange originality, because it contradicts the existing correlation between human intelligence and the things that surround us in the material world. How could man conceive of the infinite? Only when he has felt in the depths of his being the weight of the divinity which did violence to his spirit.

However, we are not speaking here of the Infinite, the infinite Being which enters into us, but of that which is infinite in relation to the world, to matter, to existence. Is it not astounding that man, made of dust, surrounded by matter, should have wished to introduce into the world the idea of the infinite? We must not despair of solving this problem, because intelligence is there in order to answer these questions. Perhaps we will know some day why, in this kingdom of matter and of the world which is under his gaze, man retained, as it were, bits of the image of the infinite.

3. *What is darkness?*

If light is matter, what can darkness be, if not also matter? It is a relative absence of that "matter-light," for an absolute absence would imply a total nonbeing. If darkness were a thing in itself, independent of light, light would not be, and all would be darkness.

But what is it, in the last analysis? It must be viewed as a logical necessity in terms of visualization, by the human being, of light. It exists in order to make light stand out, as silence makes sound stand out. For can we imagine a world made only of light? No more than a world made only of darkness, an impossible world by definition, for darkness is an aspect of being which refuses to create, whereas its very reason to be is creation.

If the world is partly made of darkness, it is because a world of pure light would be too visibly inhabited by God. But it is made only so that man might better see light. And light is made so that it may see its own brilliance. And the contrast finally awakens man from his existential slumber.

4. *Mutual relations between space and matter*

The relation between space and matter is based on the fact that there is a living cosmos. Matter and space are each a function of the other. Space, in a physical sense, is only a sort of crust on matter, because it forms around it. Matter, however, does not need space as a reality different from it: space *is* matter. We do not know where one begins and the other ends. We cannot separate them; both are manifestations of the same thing: the principle-being.

How did we reach that conclusion? Molecules, atoms, electrons, motions, mass-energy, radiation, forces in inflorescence, and forces in annihilation cannot be imagined without a medium in which to move. This space therefore exists as the other side of matter, the unknown and unperceived side of the human gaze. Atoms of matter and atoms of space form the matter-whole and the cosmos is nothing but uncondensed matter. In some part of the universe, in regions where our imagination loses itself, there exists matter in a "primitive" state, not yet dissipated, because its energy has not been transformed into heat nor felt the effect of gravity. It has therefore become neither star nor nebula, it has remained what it was *in principio*, an enormous mass of rarefied gases. For if it is true that matter, in becoming condensed, was agglomerated into stars, was it not found in a primitive state in the ether where the rarefied gases floated?

Even if we could dissect the matter of atoms surrounded by space and of the space which is inside atoms, we would never arrive at the division *ad infinitum* by which that condensed energy would become pure energy again. For in that process of division, that atom would become nothingness (or simply a space) and the final space would be a void.

Space, therefore, is something only if it persists in relation to matter, if the atoms are concentrated and become atoms again after their destruction. It is no longer anything if it is entirely divorced from matter.

But even if, theoretically, matter could be reduced to nothingness, and even if its division *ad infinitum* brings it back to the state of "space," it is something in itself, and it is necessary to give it priority over space, for space without matter is nothing. Energy is not spatial, it is exclusively material, for space is something dead within matter; it is even what will cause its death, for when it loses its essential qualities, everything will stop. And if the motion, the momentum, the expansion that is the force gushing from the heart of matter, should be extinguished, how can something remain in the cosmos? What would space alone represent? And motion? It is not matter which rolls across it; it is the motion of matter which creates the space around it and in it, space which is only the product of the forces of matter.

The mutual relationship between space and time, if compared to the relationship existing between space and matter, is superficial. Thus, in conceiving of it, Einstein merely reduced the value of time to the point of destroying it. There is no universal time, valid for the entire universe; a certain chronology is adopted by men because they live on a small planet and are not able to go too far from their habitat. What exists in the universe are small "times," moments peculiar to each group of planets or stars. But mass-energy and radiation move at random and little by little form their space and their time, which depend on matter itself.

In summary, there is a relationship between space and matter: space is an integral part of matter, it is one of its aspects. Their opposition persists as their existence develops, and Einstein reduces time to the capacity of light to overcome distance, i.e., space.

5. *Painting and space*

If we look at a picture painted by an artist, we have the impression of seeing several planes in a panorama which extends in depth; our perspective "recedes"; a window, for example, shows us a landscape beyond the walls of the room, often with an even more distant horizon, according to the painter's wishes. If his technique is good, we are prepared to swear that his picture is three-dimensional, although we know perfectly well that colors were laid on a flat canvas.

We cannot say, however, that this impression is "false"; it is true in the sense that, in the person who feels it, it fully satisfies human sensibility; ideally, emotively, it is authentic, and fits in with the perceptible world. The fact remains that our senses are grossly deceiving us.

Well, then, the false notion of things which a painting gives us is what the notion of space gives us of the world. Just as the notion of time leads us to mistaken conclusions, that of space gives us an inaccurate idea of the universe. This is all simply because time and space do not exist as realities in themselves.

6. Nonexistence of space

How can we explain the vast expanse of space compared with the small amount of existing matter? The fact is that space is also matter, and that the physical laws governing the formation of matter require that space be created around it. Thus, space is merely a consequence of matter: it is as material as matter and is its product, so to speak.

Space is not something in itself which can be separated from matter; where there is no matter, space does not exist. Just as space and time merge and amount to a single thing, space and matter are reduced to a single reality. But here there is no fusion: an element is eliminated; nothing remains but matter.

As for the ether, it is space; it is an infinitely dissolved matter, made up of elements which are scarcely material any more.

Space is a temporary necessity of matter, which tends toward a negation of space; it is an instant of matter, a boundary, a kind of veil with which it covers itself to protect itself against the assaults of nothingness, so as not to be destroyed during its endless voyage, its flight toward the endless nothingness. For matter, to stop is to die.

We will no doubt see theories arise which attempt to synthesize ether, space, and matter. In the material universe, all is matter. Unity prevails throughout, because only it gives strength, suppresses nothingness, resists destruction.

And matter prevails over that region of space which belongs to it as well.

Being and Matter

The Divisibility of Matter "ad Infinitum"

1. *The indivisible core*

If we accepted the infinite divisibility of matter, how far would we reduce it in thought? Until it became nothingness, since it is not possible to indefinitely divide something finite. To admit such divisibility would thus be to recognize either nothingness or an internally infinite matter. But if this possibility is rejected, how could nothingness exist? This way of approaching the problem of matter thus leads us to a negation of nothingness.

There exists an indivisible core in matter which has never yet been reached by the experiments of physics, and which may be an unknown form of energy. But that energy would constitute its base and would by nature be indestructible. If by a whim of the imagination we conceived of nothingness by this kind of division, how could we return to the idea of matter? Having attained nothingness, how could the parts be put back together and matter brought back from nothingness? It would be like trying to reconstruct without materials. Nothingness creates nothing, and therefore how could something return from nothingness? Nothingness accepts nothing, and therefore how could we accept a form of being simultaneous with it?

If matter is not internally divisible *ad infinitum*, it is clear that an infinity of heavenly bodies cannot exist either, and we can then state that there is an infinite God, for otherwise how could two infinities, coexisting simultaneously, be imagined? Which would be larger? The very word would lose its meaning. If God exists, He is a single infinity; any struggle between two infinities is unthinkable.

But it is necessary to point out that the problem of the divisibility of matter suddenly brought us up against the question of nothingness.

2. *What matter is*

The sorrows of the world as seen by Schopenhauer are the sorrows of matter. The anguish of Kierkegaard is rather a spiritual manifestation which rests on a material base. Whereas physical suffering is purely material and ceases with death, the being whose spirit suffers feels that that suffering is the spirit doing battle with the world of man.

Materialism, for example, is a deadly sickness, where the afflicted being dies an atheist because the darkness invades his heart. The great atheists of history had a life of suffering because they lived out the drama of matter. For a Nietzsche, a Schopenhauer, a Marx, darkness preceded light, and in destroying itself, it entailed their destruction. When nonbeing is affirmed, it obscures the function and reality of being, for matter is destined for death, and the atheist allows himself to be drawn thither.

When he accepts total death, man comes to view as real the phantoms of time, nothingness, darkness, and space. These states of absence take on bulk in the heart of the atheist (not in his thought, for it is more a matter of emotions than of concepts forged by reason). The material atmosphere which surrounds him creates "situations" in his mind which are so precise that nothingness for him becomes an irrefutable reality, the only reality possible.

The substratum of materialism is the reduction of everything and everyone to nothingness. Matter is materialism and materialism is matter.

3. *On the creation of matter*

How do things present themselves to man's consciousness? Are they a thing-in-itself or simply a creation of human thought, which would perceive them in a form entirely different from what they are in reality?

If by perception we know the world in a form different from its essence, and if what we perceive is only the form visible to our minds, why not say that matter is both a thing-in-itself and a creation of the mind? A human creation, because it really exists in our *mens* as an image captured by the senses. And yet, as an image, it is matter, but matter apprehended by the cerebral perceiving machine and reduced to barely an aspect of the thing.

Yet matter is a thing-in-itself, made up of molecules, atoms, protons, electrons, photons, mesons, neutrons, neutrines, and even other strange particles, everything that man is not able to grasp with the senses, but which is just as real as perceived objects.

In relation to man, matter assumes the role of an object, but it is a little more than merely object, because it is also something in itself and because it was created by someone who possesses the power of creation. It owes its existence to the process it has gone through, which is called creation. And it is only after having been created that it is reproduced by man in the shape and color which perception gives it. This is an act of reproduction, the raw matter of which is the image which enters into us, or which we perceive.

Then another problem occurs to us. It is the problem of nothingness in relation to matter; it arises in the human mind, because man, unable to decipher the mystery of creation except through painful effort, comes back to it as a solution of expediency.

Nothingness did not precede matter, because the creation of nothingness is something absolutely unthinkable. And if the mind does not conceive of it, it has the right to reject it; merely by admitting creation, it excludes matter-nothingness.

Finally, if we accept the preexistence of being, the being that is in a state of potentiality, the predestined being—or better, the "preessence" of being made for creation—and not of the being-for-death of Heidegger, why not also accept, at a lower level, the preexistence of matter, since it was made for man, and man could not humanly exist without it. For everything in the world of the spirit and of matter has a spiritual or objective meaning and content. To conceive of something beyond those two realms is absurd. It is tantamount to creating a third order of being.

God created man from the being He had conceived, and he brought matter into existence in order to perfect the world and the universe. But it is absurd to claim that creation was plucked out of nothingness. For nothing exists which does not stem from the act of creation. Could we accept that God, having created nothingness, would have endowed it with an essence? Man cannot imagine an essence which serves as an essence of nothingness.

And if nothingness was not created, how could it "be?"

4. *Posteriority of nothingness with respect to being*

Modern physics believes that created matter goes through processes of development, tending inexorably toward its destruction. Everything in it seems to point it toward nothingness. But what is this nothingness?

It is the state of annihilation reached by being once the route of its destiny has been terminated, and because, taking on another state, it ceases to be the being that it was, to the point of totally losing its meaning. It is a kind of nothingness posterior to matter and stripped entirely of the veils of reality. It is the natural state which follows the life of a being. It is the situation which one assumes at the end of the journey begun after the creation. It is the end, truly considered as the end. Therefore, it cannot be confused with the nothingness preceding matter, an inconsistent concept which has no reason to be.

But while it is humanly impossible to conceive, in real terms, a nothingness preceding being, the nothingness following matter is at least intelligible: man can understand the condition which matter will reach once its destiny has been accomplished. It is a state of extinction of the matter-being, and perhaps its complete transformation into another kind of being. But if we admit that the heavenly bodies can reach a state of total paralysis, having the aspect of an unformed mass, and then, despite everything, can reconstitute themselves and become a new universe as brilliant as that which we know; if there are recreations in the universe, not of new creations in the absolute sense, but regenerations preventing the total death of the cosmos, how can this optimistic vision be reconciled with the concept of nothingness?

On the other hand, if it is true that the objective world, the entire cosmos, is moving toward total extinction and unmitigated destruction, it is necessary above all to state that the matter-being, taken in itself, could not have come from nothingness, but from the creation. And man, who was not present at that creative act, will not witness the scene of annihilation either, the triumph of nothingness.

It is in creation, therefore, that we find the sole solution to the problems of the disappearance of things. The world will be reduced to dust, for this final nothingness is more similar to the dust of creation than to the nothingness of philosophy. But the human mind will never discover the reasons for that destruction, which belong to the Creator like other mysterious reasons, as, for example, those of creation. For, like the human heart in Pascal's words, the Creator has His reasons which reason knows not of.

5. *Matter, man, and the nature of things*

Matter is the substratum of things; they may be considered as things in themselves. And yet matter is nearly nothing: the more physics progresses in the study of it, the more it finds it to be immaterial, to the point of defining it as a "semi-nothingness." Things are, therefore, beings defined for nothingness, and they cannot break from that path, because they lack will, consciousness, mind, and spirit.

Man's case is different; Heidegger was mistaken in defining it as a being-for-death. This definition applies only to matter.

Matter is not what it is; it is always what it is not; it is anything but the being which man imagines it to be. At an increasing rhythm, it is always a little less than what it was; and finally, it will be reduced to destruction, or more accurately, to extinction, for its rhythm will have lost its strength. Man, on the contrary, ceases to be what he was in order to become something more. In developing himself, he is always more than what he was, and he becomes aware of this. How then could death get the better of his being, who, as "time" passes, goes ever deeper into what he is?

The contrast is striking. Nevertheless, we must not neglect the paradoxical fact that in man the two processes develop evenly. While one leads him toward death, the other makes him into the giant that he is.

6. Decay of the universe matter

Bertrand Russell sees in the second law of thermodynamics a kind of imperfection of the cosmos: "forces of decay" are acting on the heart of matter, through the transformation of K-mesons and Pi-mesons into protons, then through their elimination. We know that that which is matter cannot be called perfection, although the process of creation is perfect, and there was perfection at the beginning, because the world was the direct work of the Creator. But perfection was replaced by chance, which is to say that matter tends toward imperfection.

Nevertheless, as long as it remains matter, however imperfect, it continues to function perfectly. That is what Russell forgot. Decay does not imply the imperfection of matter, but rather signifies that matter was created with a definite goal, and not eternally.

7. On the curve of the universe

The universe is probably not "curved"; it is without shape. It is something expanding, which one may call whatever one wishes. Perhaps the cosmos we know seems curved because it is observed from earth and distorts our straight lines. But the universe of the galaxies a billion light years away—who can say that it is curved, because its shape is made up of its constantly expanding motion?

To describe it with concrete adjectives, man had first to conceive of something which resembles something unknown, and to understand the randomness which governs its inner structure.

8. The essence-being and matter

The essence-being is at the heart of matter, the world, man and the mind and spirit. Matter, however, disintegrates, at least apparently: cannot the atom be divided into more than 30 different particles?* And yet, despite everything, matter remains, for in its innermost depths, there is the essence-being, which is perhaps a vestige of its "spirituality." This is different from human spirituality, but it contains forces deriving from the Creator and giving motion and life to everything. No one can reach the innermost depths of matter, because it is a near-nothingness; it is something different even from energy or from mass-energy, it is a force which does not take up space and does not make itself felt in time.

These "forces" extend from the atom to man, then rise from man to the universe; they cause man many difficulties when he tries to draw the boundaries between the inorganic, organic, and human worlds. Everything, finally, is explained by the essence-being, the meeting place between being, which becomes man, and matter, which undoes itself in waves.

9. *Light, space, matter, and nothingness*

Light is an emanation of matter. It is both matter and radiation, and we have difficulty distinguishing these two elements in the mass-energy system, which is a single thing. Space and time are also linked to matter, which in the final analysis is their foundation: they therefore have several points in common with light, as well, were it merely their origin. But we can scarcely glimpse the outlines of this inaccessible problem: there are forces here which move in direct relationship to the force of Him who created everything that is. Why not therefore accept the spiritualization of matter along with the dehumanization of man?

10. *Cause and will*

If, in the realm of matter, the idea of cause is replaced by the notion of "chain of events," will prevails in man. But will means decision.

---

* Since 1955 scientists have discovered more than 100 elementary nuclear particles.

In the material world, we observe a chain of events, linked together, following one another in succession. But there may not exist a definite cause for each step of matter, and if matter develops, it is because there is a more general cause which is hidden from our intelligence. It is the divine hand that makes itself felt.

In the human universe, on the other hand, a living process disintegrates the determinism: the will imposes itself, in a sovereign way, because it emerges from the depths of being.

11. *Essence and cerebral matter*

In a cigarette, it is not the tobacco that is the cause of the smoke. Nor, in man, is it the brain that is the cause of thought. In the cigarette, tobacco is the raw material burned by external forces. In the human being as well, there is a kind of combustion of the brain, enabling the thought to be produced. Behind the brain lies the intellect, and there must be an unknown reaction of the brain cells when thought is born under the effect of "forces" foreign to the brain. One of those forces is called essence, and it may be called external to man, because it is in the depths of being (consciousness also has a similar origin, although it reveals itself more immediately and visibly).

And just as one may say that smoke is a product, but not a creation of tobacco, likewise thought is a product, but not a creation of the intellect, for only essence is creation. It is essence that makes the brain capable of producing thought from the cerebral matter, so that it may be possible for man to exercise his intelligence in the world.

If there were no world, we would have the immediate production of thought by the essence-being, without any need for intermediary stages, such as the personalized thought born of the human brain. But even in the presence of the world, there exists a truly immediate phenomenon in man—his consciousness; it is more spontaneous than thought, and arises at the level of being which is within each individual. Man is essentially consciousness of self.

12. *Life and matter*

The propagation of life and its development belong to matter, just as essence is proper to the spirit of man. In the same way as matter, life develops in beings which are not at the same stage. The living world possesses organic life, the very one which supports the entire human totality, and which is the "cause" of the body.

For the body exists as a result of life; it is the stage on which it unfolds. But consciousness of self, thought, and will are more immediate manifestations of essence in the living human. It is only in man that they find a focus in order to "live"; they are also less subject to evolution, to the biological and physical laws, and are only partly attached to matter, in those cases where, in the incarnate being, essence and existence come into conflict.

13. *Is life matter?*

When we use the term "life," we wish to refer to its unfolding among beings, to its vital manifestation in contact with the world. But life is matter, and it vanishes like everything that is matter, after having been accomplished through it and having been its emanation. In spite of this, it nonetheless surges from the depths of the being of matter: the "seeds" of life are of the same nature as the particles of the atomic nucleus; waves rise and fall in such insignificant fractions of time that they make us question not only time but also the stability of living matter.

But the world was created because of man. It is in this sense that man can be situated between the world and God. If man were not there, a stage would be missing between material creation and its Creator. Likewise, between matter and essence, man is there, permitting a mysterious passage between the inanimate world and life. This ambiguous situation pulls some toward a blind materialism and others toward an excessive spiritualism. Man is at the boundary of the material world and the world of life.

14. *Unpredictability of being and of the world*

Just as there are explosions and changes of orbit among the electrons in the periphery of the atom, likewise, stars and galaxies seem to spin faster and faster (around a center which we imagine to be in our galaxy) and explode in an unpredictable way, imitating the tiny world of the atom: new galaxies are then created by the transformation of gases in the cosmos and by the sudden disappearance of whole galaxies.

In the small corner of the universe which we inhabit, and which for us becomes the center of the rest, the laws of physics still seem to prevail. But what should we say of those explosions of an entirely different nature, and especially of that incredible change of orbit which occurred in the world of being when essence-being became man?

15. *Daylight and the world of essence*

The essence of matter comes from the *fiat lux*, and the essence of light is matter. At the time of the creation, unknown forces brought forth this material "clarity." But over the centuries, this light will become darkness (even though the darkness exists only as a function of light).

Man will never understand the circumstances of creation, for his imagination would lose itself in the ten, fifteen, or twenty billion years which have probably passed since then. Nor will he ever touch the essence of matter, because that essence is an unknowable light. Finally, he will not discover the secret of his own creation, that anxious impatience which God had concerning man, that burning desire which was satisfied only when the first human being came into the world from His hands.

Matter was created without the same yearning, but according to a perfect plan. And what can man say, when he gazes at the cosmos or looks inside the atom, and discovers that matter is, in fact, immaterial?

16. *The foundation of matter*

As we have said, matter has no definite shape. In its continual motion, it gives the impression of assuming the shape by which it appears to man. But we glimpse as reality an appearance quite different from matter, which is the effect of our perception, and

Berkeley was right to a certain extent in saying that matter exists only in ourselves. For it is not a being in itself, since it has no essence.

Its foundation is perhaps something "spiritual," something undetermined and unclassifiable in existential reality, something antimaterial, as if, in those deep regions, God were speaking a foreign language. Everything leads us to believe that man will not discover the true "motor" cause of the atom.

The fact is that this spiritual "something" is a near-nothingness, by its nature entirely different from the matter that stems from it and which it sets in motion. It does not have the properties of a thing, and cannot therefore be seen by man, who is capable only of grasping such realities as mass, matter, energy, radiation, and the world.

The essence of matter is there an intermediate between the human being and total existence (the world, things, phenomena), just as the essence of the human being can be considered an intermediate between God and man.

The Emotions

Analysis of Emotion

1. *The essence of emotion*

What is emotion? It comes from our being and reaches the existential human surface, but does not die upon contact with the objective world, because it is of that indestructible substance which constitutes the human substratum.

If the human being is incomprehensible, though he is not being, but merely being-transformed-into-man, it is because emotion resides within him, stronger than instinct. It is a force which comes from being, and which also permits the crystallization of the spiritual realities which come from the borders of the unfathomable.

What, for example, is music, if not an energy concentrated by emotion, and translated into notes and sounds? It is deeper if the person who composes it puts fragments of his being into it, more beautiful if it comes closer to essence. This explains the fact that we feel, but do not understand it.

In a similar manner, we know that the supreme moments of life are not those of Kierkegaardian decision. They are rather those of creation, in which emotion, breaking the chains of essence, floats to the surface of man and makes his spirit speak: essence then floats into the

165

world and makes the artist forget the world, emerging from the infinity that is interior to being; and all that is existence remains mute. To experience artistic creation is essentially to live an emotion, which is located outside the human condition and momentarily detaches one from it.

2. *Paradox of emotion*

Emotion is paradoxical, because it seems to come from nothingness. It seems to come from regions that thought is unable to reach, and of which man, on the existential level, is completely unaware of it. Through it, essence comes to the surface, but in a form so obscure that the mind cannot analyze it, and it is simply felt in the form of emotion.

We use the word "nothingness" only to refer to regions of essence, because they are not comparable to anything, while recalling that the substratum of essence is real and indestructible, and that, if this "nothingness" should intervene in the human concert, it is necessary to have tried to attain what is most perfect in man, least subject to destruction. For being became man without intervention of the human will, but it is with man's intentional aid that the being becomes a greater man, and it is emotion which awakens the being to life.

3. *Emotion and tears*

Emotion does not depend on human will. It does not derive from the intellect, but is created in the depths where human essence resides. However, it enables man to see into his being, and brings to the surfaces the forces which, in a state of potency, accumulate in the depth of being before giving birth to it.

One of the ways in which it manifests the essence of being is through tears, which are like the crystallization of profound desires, and like the *transitus* between essence and existence. For by materializing itself as tears, emotion awakens the being. But the most pathetic tear is often the one which does not flow, and does not see the light of day. It does not reach the existential surface, and remains in the temple of being. When the heart weeps, and not the eyes, it is the soul which despairs and not the being which it enlivens, and our world is changed into a kind of nothingness.

It is therefore essential for emotion to take hold of man entirely, so that it meets the other infinity, on this side, on the threshold of existence. For who can doubt that emotion is an emanation of essence? Surely not those who doubt their own existence as a result of doubting themselves!

Dialectic of Emotion and the Emotions

1. *Nothingness under its emotional prism*

The sentiment of nothingness is a negative emotion. It is a void and gives the impression of emptiness, for it is nothing: man glimpses a "nothingness" there because he feels a sentiment of anguish born of the lack of everything which he desires to possess. He aspires to be able to give birth to the world, for such is his vocation, but he feels himself frozen when he deviates from his being in mingling with the world. For if, on the one hand, he can warm up the world, it is essence which warms him up, for it alone bestows life.

In running far from himself, unsatisfied and absorbed by anguish, man loses his moral strength and invents the chimera of nothingness; it is because he despairs at not having succeeded in finding himself and in lighting the paths which lead toward himself.

2. *Love, the synthesis of emotion*

Emotion is the *raison d'ête* of love and hate, those phenomena capable of changing the course of history, because the history of civilizations is that of man. Is not war often caused by an emotion born in the sentiments of peoples, despite the vocation of men, which is to effect the synthesis of love? It is necessary to recall, however, that war is presented in the Scriptures as prior to the appearance of man, as though dating from the battle of the angels among themselves, so that man would be born with the sign of aggression on his forehead.

He is not only love, therefore: he is love and struggle. His emotion, born in the heart of being, is capable of wounding the heart of the world; the more man perfects his presence in the world, the more wars multiply. But let us rather speak of love, which is the true synthesis of emotion. Man loves the beloved object, but it is the being which gives the capacity to love; it is through the being that his capacity to love is nourished, and becomes that light which lights the human mass. The human being, therefore, is not reduced to his emotions, any more than the theater is reduced to the scenes that are acted in it. In any case, even if love could be reduced to an emotion, hate would be reduced to nothingness. And man would remain the being that he is in himself, a reality not reducible to emotion, either of love or of hate.

3. *Man's irreducibility to emotion*

Man endures everything. He persists during life despite the turmoil of his own inner life, despite the blows of existence and of the objective world. He maintains himself after death, and even eternity will not destroy him! If nothing destroys being, what an immense potency it represents, that which God wished to make indestructible, and which was meant to last longer than emotion and time: He counterposes to them his being, which will be pure being and immortal spirit.

Man's weakness, however, lies in the fact of having been created. Created in a moment of deep emotion by the Creator, he was the emotion of love, as Pascal says, an emotion which was the desire to see one of His works embodied—that is to say, a quite different emotion from that which is felt by man, something greatly superior, and yet emotional. And because of this origin, the being which has taken on a human shape has become fragile, uneasy, dissatisfied. It has lowered itself to being a man, a giant no doubt, but a giant who would be born a child, and would become a titan only after having made within himself the transformations necessary for a Promethean vocation: to cultivate his essence, while taking care not to stray from earth.

Let man not wish to become god. Even if he rises above everything and above himself, as an existential being, let him nevertheless fear a fall as dizzying as his flight.

4. *The emotion of flight*

Matter runs and does not get tired: a comet, if it comes in contact with unknown shores, nonetheless follows a blind path, because it follows the immutable laws of physics. And it always becomes a little more different than what it was before.

Man lives. And, symmetrically, he becomes always more than what he already was: he accumulates everything that he keeps from life, that emotional matter, that substratum which we call essence. He may appear to change, to become another being and another man, but he does not cease to be what he is in himself, and if he adds new elements to his being, nothing alters its substance. His life is like a flight, but what difference does it make if the surroundings have changed, provided the bird remains the same?

Man changes into a being which remains immutable; the being is transformed into man, without losing its characteristics of being.

5. *Is a dream emotion?*

If a dream is the synthesis of what man, during the day, has felt or wished to experience, it is probably, although in an indirect way, the product of emotional reactions in the human being.

If time, being matter, is not able to measure immaterial emotion, it is therefore unusable also in the realm of dreams, where the scenes change with an abruptness defying the human gaze. All that seems to have lasted for hours has happened within minutes.

For in dreaming, man transcends matter, with the help of emotion. He surpasses time, he realizes himself, by subordinating everything that represents the material in him: the objective world lives in his dream only as a memory.

Emotion-Time

1. *Emotion and the concept of time*

Times arises in an emotional context: man uses it to fix his place in the vastness composed of unbounded spaces; he clings to time out of fear of the infinite. He does not fear matter because his feet rest on it. But since space goes beyond what he can see, he sees it as "a torn piece of eternity." If there were no space, man would not conceive of time, but he believes that by seizing the reins of time, he will reach the nontemporal more easily, and can rid himself of matter which holds him on earth.

He thus conceives of time in a profound state of emotion, when his essence, in an explosion of feeling, comes into contact with the objective, existential world; he sees the world, he sees that mad rhythm which drives the cosmos, that incessant rhythm which cannot be followed by his thought, and the concept of time is born from motion, from matter, from the world and from human memory.

But if his thought is reduced to an emotion, man is not reduced to it; and though he is essence rather than emotion, he is not reduced to essence, either, from which emotion derives: he remains himself, and, in the process, time is first emotion, and only then conceptual "time."

2. *Emotion and headlong flight*

Man during his lifetime feels a strange sensation, an emotion born

171

of flight; he despairs because he moves away from himself and from his center, which is being. He rushes toward a beyond which he does not know, and which provokes an incurable anguish in him. We may compare him to a comet which must reach places beyond the world. In this panicky flight, the human being would still be able to guarantee his own identity, thanks to the strength of his essence, that "incessant murmuring of his inner life" which Bergson calls duration. But in the emotion of flight, man wanders in a disorganized fashion, without knowing where he is going and without being able to stop, in an interminable journey which is rather a coming and going.

A lifetime is a minuscule grain of sand on the shore of the cosmos, compared to the history of the galaxies. However, man, lost amidst the mass of the universe, has been able to adapt time to the reality of his existence, his life, and himself. The important thing is not to make time a reality in itself.

3. Emotion of things past

Death is more the loss of something than something in itself. We should point out the close relationship that exists between death and that human emotion which existentialism calls "rooting" and in which we can recognize the nostalgia for the world, linked in man's heart to the fear of death. This nostalgia anticipates the real loss and appears when the being foresees the disappearance of that which is dear to him. He often carries the memory of simple things, like a face, a look, a house, daily habits; and it is all stronger in that it has a conscious base and rests on our essence (whereas the instinct of preservation is only our organism, which rebels and calls on the material forces of our existential being).

Nostalgia is emotion, it is a "thing" which belongs to being, but which elevates and ennobles us, even if it sometimes depresses and wounds us.

4. Emotion and rhythm

Just as rhythm gives a cadence to matter, emotion can serve as a rhythm for being, for in the realm of being, nothing is really measured, and essence is manifested only by emotion, which gives an idea of what is going on in our soul. In defining that "incessant motion of our inner life" as a duration, Bergson wanted to detach it from the physical laws which dominate growth and the life of things existing in the world; and, indeed, it rebels against laws, rhythms, and "times." Our being, when it speaks, does not do so in a language which can be reduced to numbers: it makes us perceive spontaneous explosions, which are accidents impossible to predict.

In periods of calm, we can live through moments of silence, during the day and especially at night, during those profound sleeps which are paralyses of our inner life. The true image of our essence will always be distorted if it is subject to time, for it is found less in our physiological life than in our emotional life. But that life is comparable to the explosions by which matter loses its energy and increases its mass, or vice versa. The law of quanta governing the atom might well be applied to our inner life, freeing the life of our emotions from all methodical calculations.

5. *Emotional foundation of the past*

What is time, in relation to our inner life, if not its concretization in existential terms? And what role does time play in the world, in relation to our being which is not there, since it is only the existential man who lives in the present, the past, and the future? Does it perhaps aid in the crystallization of our inner life, in face of the past, which has entered into it, and the present, which escapes it, and does it give an idea of the rhythm governing the vital unfolding of matter? But perhaps also the word "crystallization" is poorly chosen; because time neither represents nor measures the variations of our inner life, it is not able to hold back the vital force which is in our essence.

It is wrongly thought that one is unable to "stop time," as though it were something that moves, a car rolling across the spaces of existence, a reality. No one, however, would say that time is a being that as its development progresses, as it passes, becomes more than it is: it is always what it was before, something that does not change and does not acquire new forms.

Rather, it is our inner life which is constantly evolving, searching for what is infinitely more than us, and which nonetheless attracts us.

But Heidegger wonders if time is not "a horizon of man"! Let us recognize, however, that this question occurs in the last phase of his work: he seems to base his entire system on time and temporalization, that is, on the realization of man thrown into existence. And it is useful to note that Heidegger reproaches Bergson for his attempt to spatialize time. He is really not far from admitting, on this point, that time is a real entity, and also from refusing to see in it only man himself, whereas the need for a chronology is an echo from the depths of being, which reaches the surface of existence in the form of emotion, but cannot be reduced to objective terms.

Time is more man than man is time. Certain philosophies have exaggerated its role in human life to the point of conceiving of man only from its standpoint. We prefer, rather, to define it as a human phenomenon of an emotional nature, like the frustration of a simple, deep emotion, of a positive emotion which man is unable to objectify: the reduction to material terms of that which, in the human being, is the most immaterial—remembrance. The consternation man feels when he contemplates his past stems from the fact that time is an incommunicable emotion; it seems to crystallize in him and makes him want to delimit his life, by separating his past from his present, but it nevertheless does not become a being when it is reflected on the world. For present and past have meaning only for man, who lives through them; they are reduced to man's emotions. For man lives through "his" time, but it is being which creates "the" emotional time which is impossible to objectify, which lives as the past in everyone.

For the past is an already crystallized emotion which is part of the human substratum, and to destroy that element would be to destroy parcels of being, to prevent it from becoming human. But if time does not destroy man, neither can man erase in himself the traces of the past, the life already lived.

Berdyaev, in *Five Meditations on Existence,*[1] paradoxically assures us that the past never existed. What existed yesterday was of the present, it was another present, and the past does not exist as such except in the present.

We reply that it is not the existence of the past which counts, it is the fact that being does not die. The separately experienced manifesta-

---

[1] *Cinq Méditations sur l'Existence.* Paris: Editions Aubier Montaigne, 1936, p. 137.

tions are to life what chords are to a symphony, and it is the integral man who lives his past and his present. Human life in stages is made up of extratemporal emotions, each with its own characteristic and momentum. The past is the emotion which grazed existence and disappeared from the world, that is, ceased to exist with the warmth that was peculiar to it, to return to the heart of being. It does not entirely disappear, and in that sense, Berdyaev is right in saying that the past exists as such in the present of today. Even if it does not exist, it at least survives in the depths of being, and the separately experienced emotions constitute a whole which synthesizes the spirituality by which man lives.

6. *Emotive consciousness of time*

Having established the basis of the past as emotional expression, let us consider other aspects of emotion-time.

In looking back at the past, we see what is capable of emotions in being; the present and the future, rather, place one in the presence of sentiments about what one is and will be. Of course, man must always be what he is because his essence is not transformed. However, when he comes into direct contact with the world he becomes temporalized, even if that temporalization flows more from his life in full expansion than from the moments which man needs in order to realize himself as an existential being.

The consciousness of time as defined by Heidegger is the emotive consciousness of something which does not exist as a thing-in-itself, but which is present in human thought as the reflection of the strong emotion resulting from contact with reality, and from the uncertainty man feels toward his future. This is one more proof that, far from representing a being, time is the product of an emotional state which takes hold of man, but in reality awakens in the depths of being (which became man without the intervention of time). Fear of the future is also a reflection of the contingencies of life in the world, for if time were a "law," man would have nothing to fear from the future, and could foresee it as the astronomers calculate the path of a star. To the contrary, if it belongs to his inner life, which manifests itself in the form of emotions, man will feel himself invaded by certainties and doubts which gnaw at him and push him to despair. If man does not know his future, it is because he does not know himself.

But, in the last resort, the past and present cannot be separated from the future, since human life, made up of an infinity of emotions, is nonetheless a whole. It is an uninterrupted succession of acts, or rather of elements comparable to isolated notes of which a symphony is composed, and which, in the last analysis, stem from the inner depths of being.

7. *Emotion-time and Heidegger's temporalization*

Heidegger's *Dasein* has in it the power to become the future, to come into being. But to be what? Perhaps itself? But then, why is it only the past, if it contains within itself the capacity to be the future? For the past, before being such, must have been the future of a more distant past! But according to Heidegger, time is identical to the *Dasein*, and being is the past only if it is the future. Still, this logic is valid only if the being is alive. Right at the moment of death, since it does not threaten to become the future, according to Heidegger's logic, it can no longer be the past either, and all of its lived history falls apart—the being would simply cease to be. It is quite possible that by creating the notions of past being and future being, Heidegger may have given another name to Aristotle's potency and act (for potency is nothing so long as it has not become an act).

However, the supreme characteristic of being is that it *is*, and it *is* independently of temporalization, as well as the act and potency, for the last two are manifestations, however primary, of the being itself, and someone will have to execute them: that someone is being. Then we enter the realm of essence: being does not go from potency to the act thanks to the Heideggerian *Dasein*, by transporting itself from the past to the future. Potency and act are phases of the being which becomes man.

Nor can it be said that the past emerges from the future, for it is not the future which is formed, nor the past which was formed; it is being which becomes the future or became the past. The future is the logical consequence of being, which will continue to be in the future, because it holds within itself the capacity to be a being in the future and to continue in the future as the person that it was in the past. Man is future because he has (already) been past, he is past because he is something more than even future and past. Let us go further: man is not exactly a future at the present moment, he will become future, he is not future in himself. He will achieve being because prior to that, he is already what he is.

Heidegger is correct is saying that "temporality is not a being, and would not be one because it is temporalized," for temporality *is* only as a result of man, and is temporalized only during the existence of an individual: it is only one aspect of man during his lifetime.

Dialectic of Emotion and of Essence

1. *Meaning of the being; essence and emotion*

According to N. Hartmann, instead of the question of "the being as being," Heidegger asked the question of "the meaning of being." But all ontology is blind if it does not solve the first of these two problems, and in appealing to the meaning of being, Heidegger is content to reduce being to time. For the meaning of being is nothing other than the meaning of man; it is man, who, in face of the world, takes his true place. But it must be recalled that emotion plays a role in the inner life of man. Thanks to emotion, he achieves the limits of plenitude. And precisely, emotion is a manifestation of essence, an integral part of being; it is its ability to achieve itself and to live while feeling life and the world in which it lives. So that it is above all the being itself which gives a meaning to being.

Let us look at the German philosopher's reasoning: the "meaning" of anything must be that same thing which has become a being, and which must have a way of being. Without it, it is nothing. Thus, one should ask not only about the meaning of being but also the "being of meaning." We reply that while it is true that every being must have a way of being (which is one's way of behaving in the world during one's life and existence), this way of being can have no other origin than essence-being. But it is emotion which crystallizes that meaning required by being and adopted because of it.

On the other hand, the meaning which each individual human being takes on for others is different from that which he has for himself, and by which, however, he presents himself to others as the being he is. For without this last meaning, would the very act of appearing to others be possible? The being would initially be empty of meaning, and would not acquire one except as a function of others. Without that external intervention, he would be nothing! Let us recall, therefore, that it is being which gives reality to every person, that without man's essence, he would be nothing, and that it is in this way that the schema of the integral human being is completed: being-man-existence.

The meaning of being, which, according to Heidegger, is that same being's reason for being, would therefore above all be the meaning of the existence being, its course in life and in existence, its way of leading its life, a way of being which would encompass all the ways of being that it has successively known. For essence-being and existence-being—each within its limits—act on the whole of the integral being.

As for the "being of meaning," it is necessarily merged with it, for meaning comes after being, and consequently draws from it the totality of what it is.

2. *Emotional disturbances*

The reestablishment of the equilibrium lost in the original Fall is a task in which man can triumph only through the values of Christianity. Without them, man is an incomprehensible being, unknown to himself, evading the most stringent laws of existence, for nothing makes him really contingent, not even the contingency he creates for himself.

Emotion, which is the very essence of life, can sometimes destroy being by driving it to insanity. For insanity is the negation of the self and the destruction of consciousness; the madman is certain of everything except the fact that he represents the being that he really is. Is it because he knows the meaning of nothingness and converses with the phantoms of the void?

With the rupture of equilibrium, the unity of being is broken, and the light that shines on the "sleeping world" can destroy the man whose emotions have grown disproportionately, making him lose the power of comprehension and of self-awareness. He imagines himself to be a being that he will never be, and thus he will no longer be anyone, becoming a being which has lost its being. Is this not a very picture of nothingness!

3. *Essential origin of emotion*

Human emotional time does not measure the smallest interval when the being goes from essence to existence. There is a certain resemblance between being and existing, so that one may confuse them and reduce them to a single term. But there is never a complete fusion between them, and they remain one only because of an interchange between their manifestations, the one remaining on the right bank and the other on the left bank of the river which may serve as an image of human life. Perhaps it is thought, perhaps it is emotion which constitutes the essence of life, or perhaps it is another unknown reality? In any case, it is from the interchange described above that man stems.

He is the synthesis of opposing or superimposed elements. But his unity appears in an unequivocal way; his elements are not merged, but could not exist by themselves, and each of them by itself cannot represent the integral human being. For man's life as a being existing in the world goes along with an internal life in which the flame of essence is fed by the fire of emotion, itself a reflection of the internal universe.

In existential life, emotion exists also, in the form of emotional states which are nothing but the cooled remnants in which we find the recollection, turned into living matter, of that ardent emotion peculiar to the realm of being.

4. *Dialectic of essence and of emotion*

Is the essence of the human being a kind of concrete synthesis of his emotions? Reason, because it does not grasp that which is of essential origin in emotional phenomena, tries to reduce them to itself, as though man were merely reason! To the contrary, existential man is closer to the depths of being without cold reason than with it.

Emotions are quite varied, and owe their diversity to the very nature of the human being, an inexhaustible source of spiritual energy. But where is the primary emotion, the motor force of so much spirituality? Certainly, in human essence, the foundation of any *ego*. And it is when emotion reaches the surface of existence that man can be transported to those regions. He would not arrive there otherwise, neither by "the simplicity of the primitive experience," of which Marcel de Corte speaks, nor by "the wonderment, the unfamiliarity with the fact of existing, the bite of the real, the unverifiable in oneself," of which G. Marcel speaks. That philosopher further calls these phenomena "a transportation to the natural plane of the *fides de non visis* of Grace." We say, rather, that it is concentrated emotion which makes essence, and if we were to discover the nature of life, we would surely know the deepest secrets of being.

But all of this escapes our knowledge, despite our insistence on grasping the ungraspable, for, as Kierkegaard says, the paradox of thought is to try to discover something which cannot itself think. This passion of thought basically remains present everywhere in it, and also in that of the individual, insofar as, when he thinks, he is not only himself.

This ungraspable primary emotion appears (only to the eyes of the soul!) as a spiritual emanation of high value, which is never complete, because it is the essence of all spirituality, the supreme foundation of being, and because God Himself created man in a state of infinite emotion.

But after it comes a whole series of emotional explosions, by which emotion passes into existence. It was in a similar manner that matter went from inanition to motion; its initial force was also of emotional origin. Inversely, therefore, if the universe should perish, and if man also (become pure being) should again find himself in Eternity, one can likewise say that his death is emotion, that it is the supreme emotion of his adventure in life. The emotion of the Being is above all the emotion of being: it takes hold of each being when he becomes what he is.

Epilogue: Sentiment of Death and Emotion-Time

The image of time develops in the human intellect when one sees a loved being disappear. And yet, the death of another is not the true emotion of death, which is for each person the wait for his own disappearance. But it is a normal psychological reaction in man to then turn toward himself: because of his bereavement, he is in a good position to see the temple of his being with the eyes of the soul.

If, on the other hand, he pushes the thought away from his being, he loses himself in the life of the world and is surrounded by shadows, such as contingency, pain, grief, and time, too, among others! Why include time here, and mingle its false sensation of reality with emotions felt outside of it? Because the world, moving inexorably toward death, cloaks itself in deceptive elements, and the image of time is created in the man placed before or within this drama.

Another idea, however, would better explain to man that idea which he calls time and which took hold of him at the moment of the emotional impact of death: that of rhythm. But how can rhythm, since it is life, be reconciled with thoughts of the wait for an imminent end? How to substitute it for time?

It is necessary to remember that the rhythm ceases, at least in the world of existence, upon the death of each being. In this final trance, it becomes in any case so strong that man loses consciousness of the objective world and is transformed into a new man. But infinitely better than the dead idea of time, it fits in with that cluster of sensations, of emotion felt and borne by man. For time was invented by man, and rhythm was willed by God.

When man enters Eternity, the rhythm which was installed in him is totally quelled.

But time or rhythm—all is emotion.

Dialectic of Being and of the World

The Interaction of Existence

1. *Knowledge of the Material Object*

How does the "cognitive subject," which is the spirit embodied in the world, know the object, which is matter, asks Heidegger in the course of his search for nothingness: "Does it jump from its internal sphere and enter into another sphere, foreign and external to it?" In reality, man is also matter, he is the synthesis of matter and of spirit, so that he can drive his thought, immaterial though it may be, into the heart of the material world.

However, man knows things by their shape, which he half perceives, and when the infinite is in front of him, he is submerged by his thoughts, which led Malebranche to conclude: "God shows man his smallness in the simple facts of life." Matter, however, is inferior to his spirit, it can be known by him without being able to know him, and cannot therefore be raised to the status of another "sphere," equal to that of the creative spirit (for it is the spirit which creates the image of matter).

185

And if, on the other hand, they assure us that the brain is matter, it is necessary to answer that it is not the brain which conceives the idea: it is the theater in which the drama of thought unfolds, but what generates thought is the spirit, the light of the being which becomes man—in a way, moreover, which we do not know.

Matter, the other "sphere," is a semi-nothingness. What counts is the human power to know it, in whatever form. The subject-object problem therefore boils down to knowledge. Every day the torn veils which conceal matter from the eyes of the spirit fall away.

2. *Man's spirituality and materiality*

The world was created for man, but each man also creates his world; without this power "of creation," he would not be in the world, he would not understand it. What belongs to humanity as a whole is the external world, a dead thing. But the individual man who comes into existence in order to live and fulfill himself as a being, creates a world in the course of this process of self-improvement; he creates it as something belonging to him, out of external facts which cease to be lifeless realities, and which fuse with the human being.

However, in certain cases of ecstasy, man is able to abstract from himself any influence which matter, flesh, and the world may exert on his existential being, and to emerge completely from it. These states of sublime elevation of the spirit scarcely allow the body to be a body.

As for the opposite situation, which makes us say that a being has lost his soul and now lives only in a vegetable state, we may ask if that is not an empty formula: every human being, however animalized he may be, will retain at least some vestiges of his soul.

But we must recognize that these two extreme cases are, in any event, hypotheses of a rather theoretical sort, and that the union of the body and the soul is so intimate that one can hardly think of disassociating them.

3. *Independence of the cognitive subject*

We should assume two categories of knowledge on the part of the subject: a possibility of immediately knowing immaterial "facts" and perception of an object having a physical reality through the medium of the senses.

Immediate knowledge usually concerns the immaterial world. Consciousness of self, for example, occurs without the aid of the sensory apparatus. The creation of an idea may also take place without outside things having been perceived to serve as a sample or a model for it; the idea is an immaterial emanation from the creative force of being, and a manifestation of it as being. But it gives the being a chance to manifest itself in the objective world, enabling essence to shed its rays on the world of existence (hence, moreover, the strength of ideas, which are sometimes capable of changing the face of the world).

However, once it is accepted that the subject can know certain realities (of an immaterial nature) without the aid of the senses, why not recognize the possibility of a subject independent of its object? The question arises under two different aspects: knowledge by the subject without an object and existence of the subject-being without object-being.

The subject-being exists in the world, where it awakens to life and leads its existence. But can it develop independently of matter? Existence is necessarily existence in the world, and if we find in it a constant opposition between the subject and the object, we must conclude, beyond any doubt, that the subject does not exist independently of it.

But being is not only of this world, and was not made to live only on this earth. The subject, as pure being, when it ceases to be a subject in order to be a being, can be and act without any relationship to an object, whereas the latter, on the contrary, draws all of its significance from its relationship to the subject. This follows from the superiority of being over matter. The opposite would imply that being needs the object in order to assert itself as something in itself: it would no longer be being, but matter.

4. *Irreducibility of thought to perception*

To claim that man is matter is to give the world the role of a king of creation, and attribute to thought an external cause, rather than conceiving of it as stemming from the depths of being. Human comprehension would become the exclusive result of the perception of images. The world, conceived as the first cause of thought, would be the supreme power in creation.

Man, as a conscious being, would be reduced to existence, for he would be manifested only within its limits. The world would be left to assume itself with a mob of marionettes.

5. *From the smallness of the universe to the grandeur of being*

If the spirit-man rises infinitely above matter, how can the being which becomes man be kept within a minuscule world? How can an immaterial nature, which is self-sufficient, be reconciled with another of an opposite kind, unconscious and obeying physical laws? Above all, how can the former be placed in a universe in which only appearances are visible?

This difficult juxtaposition is the consequence of the Fall of the spirit-being, which became man and human individual. Man feels the difficulty of delimiting the realms of essence and existence, as a result of his very situation as an embodied spirit. But because existence is more tangible and he receives everything from it—because on the other hand, essence is hidden as a result of the Fall, in the secret of being, it is necessary for man to break the chains of matter and of existential manifestations, which put him under all kinds of pressure.

But the man who inhabits this world peopled with appearances is a fallen being. The world transforms him and makes him human, but nonetheless leaves him traces of spirituality, which it is essential for him to develop in order to fulfill himself.

It is necessary, therefore, for man to find beauty, harmony, grandeur in the world, and for the abode of man to have dimensions which at least do not further reduce the fallen spirit, but to the contrary, help it to perfect itself. That is why the universe is large: the majesty of the cosmos is explained in terms of the grandeur of being.

6. *The human being and full reality*

"I cannot really stand aside from the universe," even in thought, G.

Marcel declares.[1] He adds: "We are involved in Being, and it is not in our power to leave it: more simply, *we are*, and our whole inquiry is just how to place ourselves in relation to the plenary Reality."[2] A statement of the same kind is found in Heidegger: "As surely as we shall never comprehend absolutely the totality of what-is, it is equally certain that we find ourselves placed in the midst of what-is, and that this is somehow revealed in totality."[3]

Man exists in this world, and could not exist outside of his environment, for, outside of the matter-world culminating in infinity, in which he is allowed to present himself as an existence-being, he would not be able to live. That is a *sine qua non* of existence, convincing us that man is imaginable only in the context of the cosmos, of which he is an integral part, and from which he cannot escape by physical means. There is no other possible nature that can encompass human reality.

And yet, the more we are tied to the world of things, the greater will be our need of escape, the stronger will be our tendency to free ourselves from the yoke of matter, from the domination of the world-being, which drags us toward nothingness, subjecting us to a drastic process of despiritualization. A single door will lead beyond the material environment—spirituality. For man, as a being, transcends that reality which the spirit knows and penetrates, but which does not know the being entirely. If it were an integral part of the total materiality, this would mean:

a) an existence comparable to an abyss, where man would be drawn by forces alien to him and logically superior; his life would be reduced to a march toward nothingness;

b) total materiality would be the first cause, the generating and motor force of being in general, including the human being.

But there is something that transcends total materiality—creation. If there were no creative act preceding that reality, it would be its own creator. Let us add that if such an act precedes it, it also precedes man, who of all beings, is the most precious, having origins outside of

---

[1] *Being and Having: An Existential Diary*. Gloucester, Mass.: Peter Smith, 1976, p. 19.

[2] *Being and Having*, p. 35.

[3] Martin Heidegger, *Existence and Being*. Chicago: Henry Regnery Company, 1949, p. 363.

existence. However, how can we not recognize that, because of those very origins, being is capable of elevating itself above that reality which enslaves it?

Still, as a cognitive subject, it will not be separated from its object, for subject and object, although in constant opposition, define one another. And the subject-object relationship will have so much importance in the end for the very personality of each person, that we can consider being to be marked by them in its very structure.

As long as he is in the world, man will carry its weight on his shoulders. Total materiality surrounds him. However, while he must live his earthly life with his feet on the ground, he must at least know how to stand upright.

7. Struggle betweeen man and matter

It was necessary for man to awaken matter from its sleep so that we might reach the current phase of human history. It is scarcely any time at all that man has lived in this world. The world was reduced to dead matter which no one had ever yet looked at, and which was saving its breathable atmosphere for the living species destined to occupy it. But man grew weary of the earthly breezes. He likes to fill his lungs only with oxygen in the air; Cain's crime proves that the smell of blood also tempts him.

Man's struggle against his brothers should not, however, be considered an episode in his war against the entire material world. We can say that he won the first round of that battle, for we are in the midst of the atomic era, the proof that man dominates matter, from which he has wrested its secrets. But as for the final victory, the question remains open. How long will man maintain his superiority? And who will benefit from it?

Certainly not the man that man is on earth, made of flesh and blood, possessing an intellect, taking on an existence: it would be necessary for a new man to be created, one fully immersed in his essence, which alone, because it is light, will end this bloody battle and enable the integral human being to rise above the human, the world and matter.

But in order that man may awaken being with all his strength, he will first have to climb back down the ladder of existence: from existence to man, and from man to being. If he does not do so, he will succumb to the forces of the world, the elements of which are in open battle against human values. This effort, coming from man depending solely on him, can be made by him only out of a sense that if he does not do it, he will end in death.

Once more it becomes necessary to discern in each individual that succession of levels in which the principle and the true aim are called essence, and the temporary consequence, existence.

8. *The world seen from within*

The world is an eternal incitement to struggle (the word *eternal* meaning only something uninterrupted and incessant, like a waterfall).

This is because matter itself is in motion, and it leads man to see, feel, think and conceive of the world: his thought moves only as a result of impulses from the outside. A difficult, but unavoidable situation: it is the consequence of the original Fall, and it is a kind of anathema weighing on him.

9. *Dynamism of the human being*

Man is dynamism, but this dynamism results both from externally caused impulses and from forces surging within him, comparable to the gravitational force of the planets, independent of other men and of the energy existing in the outside world: they stem above all from his freedom.

If history is the story of human accomplishments in the world, why could it not be explained by the collision of man's dynamism with the forces of matter? Man in the world, dominating matter or dominated by it, constitutes the framework of historical events. He influences the unfolding of history as a pure being, as a generator of ideas, as sovereign will and spirituality. But also, as existence—man, in a direct, let us say material way: since his spiritual influence is distant, the materialists do not see it. But since the spiritualists see nothing else, they also sin by excess, for the influence of the spirit is felt through the existence-being, through individual humans.

Finally, it is necessary to emphasize that human dynamism is not uncontrollable: it follows a direction and goes toward the future. And that is why the most distant civilizations have left traces of human action, the product of the creative dynamism which lived at that time and that did not end even with the disappearance of individuals, for it is transmitted from generation to generation, defying time and death.

10. *Material environment of fallen man*

The placing of man within matter was the greatest punishment that he could have been given. His Fall in the world is the consequence of an anathema: even in order to know himself, he is forced to begin with his environment. But let us remember that man is something more than an inhabitant of Earth: he *was* before being born there. Thus, one might imagine a different existential stage on which man could exist and live (to exist meaning rather to undergo the contingencies which man creates as long as he is in the world; to live meaning to develop in a given direction, according to an uninterrupted rhythm).

But in any case, man thinks, dreams, exists, despairs in terms of the world, having as a point of departure, even for knowledge of himself, this world which appears to him as private property. And whether or not we view our planet as man's exclusive habitat, we feel the imperious need to look for something more solid, more substantial, where man can affirm himself as the being he is, superior to the world. This can only be the principle of man, that principle-being that he himself is in face of the world, where he appears as the only pure being.

11. *Conquering the world*

It is by conquering the world that man fulfills himself. Even though he lives surrounded on all sides by objective reality, he possesses within himself sufficient forces to annul within himself the influence of the world on the shaping of his own nature, as an integral being.

When he is able to destroy the world in himself, he will have unblocked the road to the maxim "Know thyself" of the Greek sages. For matter is like a wall which stands between man and his being.

Moreover, it acts on the very structure of being through man, who is an integral part of the integral human being. To force oneself to resist this contamination and not become animalized is a task that defies will, and the human being will not become integral if, in that struggle, he does not win the "decision," in the Kierkegaardian sense of the word.

Strength of will is specifically human: the planets travel distances without will, and decision, in that realm where there is no freedom, implies a different will, the sovereign Will which guides them. In the human drama, to the contrary, decision is an objective concretization of an act or of a volitional force, it is a manifestation of the will which attains its goal, which has been achieved. This victory is unimaginable without consciousness of self; only a being that understands itself as a being may command and execute.

But if the world is a thing without life or consciousness, it could nevertheless win a kind of decisive victory, a negative one, by contaminating the human being profoundly, by deforming his nature. Thus the Creator decided: it is one of the possible forms of punishment for fallen man.

12. *Freedom of the world*

The world penetrates man, like a kind of vapor, by images and memories, which break up the unity of being and promote the existence-being at its expense, which was made for the world as the world is made up for it. The existent is in its entirety adapted to the environment (be it physical or spiritual), the totality of external facts in contact with each. The nature of the body, likewise, is shaped by the physical and chemical influences, by the biological whole.

And yet man does not belong to matter, nor to his existence, since it is only a degree in the scale of his being; and he does not belong to himself either, but to the One who made him. And it is precisely for that reason that man must expel the world from himself, in order to truly fulfill himself in the course of his life in the world. But for the most part, we see freedom in the slavery caused by the world; pleasure in its sorrows; joy in its tears; delight in its anguish—a total reversal of the values intuitively known by the human heart.

As for our fellow man, it is not through him either that we can acquire true consciousness of ourselves, as certain existentialists assert. Others barely manage to awaken what is slumbering in us, our tendencies, our emotions, our personality; but never being, the only reality capable of making an integral human being in our person. For it is only through being that a given man *is*: he must therefore free himself by his own efforts.

13. *Man and the world*

It is therefore urgent to wrench man away from the world, and even more to extirpate the world from man, this world which creates anguish, arising from the notion of nothingness, but, in a vicious circle, bringing to life that same nothingness, the destroyer of the spiritual universe in which being is located. In reality, the human being ardently desires the infinite, but it is first necessary for him to make the effort to become conscious both of his essence and of his existence. No sooner is that effort made than man has already climbed a rung above the abyss which he himself dug, while the world was opening another abyss in his mental universe.

Kierkegaard, for example, asks in terror: "Why am I this isolated individual, this particular man, here and now?" And Heidegger echos him: "When man awakens to conscious life, he is already in the world, as though someone had already thrown him there. Who? No one. Why? There is no reason." These men do not see that nothingness is the product of fear in man, who, along with faith, has lost the moral courage necessary to face what his eyes do not recognize, and what makes his thought waver. This fear is in reality only a trembling before being!

Tear man away from the world, and we destroy (or at least soothe) the anguish that torments him. Let us chase despair from the human heart, when we feel its weight, by the strength of that wind of the immortal truths of the spirit and the transcendental values of being. Let us detach man from the world, for the world-nothingness-fear cycle is making a growing wound in the soul. To rehumanize man (after having de-existentialized him), to again make of him an integral man let us penetrate our being! For in its temple are perceived the breath and the presence of the Divine Being.

14. *Depersonalization of contemporary man*

The principle cause of the current crisis is not overpopulation. It is rather the sensation felt by modern man of being lost by living according to the rhythm of crowds. In the big cities, he is conscious of living in the herd, of thinking like his group, of feeling like the mass, which gives him the direction of his life and even decides which emotions he "ought" to have. The Group teaches him everything, and science itself, as Huizinga remarked, has moved away from its center, which was man. Man, for his part, has lost the habit of thinking, because a being superior to him thinks in his place and makes him into a kind of robot in the hands of the multitude.

We are therefore witnessing a displacement of being: that which has its usual place in the human person escapes from this internal world which has let itself be invaded by the materiality of the outside, and has been completely taken over by the existential man; yet this man is nothing but a portion of what we really represent!

The dignity of being, expelled by man, seems therefore to have been usurped by society. But it is first and foremost on the individual level that we must try to repair this disorder. Each person must strive to find his essence. For this, it is necessary to get away from the crowd and from the world, and plunge once again into being.

Inquiry into the Principle-Being

Being and Death

1. *Human corpses*

St. Augustine defines the corpse as something that exists and does not live; let us explain that this thing exists as long as it is materially present, and will cease to exist when it has become dust, becoming transformed into something extinct, incapable of representing anything, not even a body. Moreover, the body, even when alive, has no being, but it participates in the human drama, at least in a secondary role, since the body enables man to exist as a living being.

The corpse, on the other hand, plays no role: even the fact of having been a body does not give it any reality, since the body exists only because of the human being living in it. Thus, the corpse is nothing; death makes it nothing, while man become spirit.

And what about the resurrection of the dead? Will the corpse be reanimated? Certainly not! What will be resuscitated are men: their corpses will continue not to exist.

2. *The image of the dead*

In speaking of being and of music, we were saying that it is only after death that being is fulfilled, for death destroys in it whatever is material, existing, and human. The being which dies (because existence and world die in it) at the same time becomes itself and a new being.

It is significant to recall that the most striking recollection, the true portrait of a man (whose appearance changes during his lifetime), is that which dates from shortly before his death: the face as it appeared at the approach of death can give a definitive image to posterity. Is that not a kind of confirmation of the idea that the being is achieved when the man dies? Only then, he *is*, *per omnia saecula*. And his recollection remaining in the memory of men is what remains of the existential in him, by assuming the shape he had when he ceased to be the man he was.

3. *Man's death*

Death does not belong to the world; it is not of the material world. Everything that happens to man, however, pertains to matter, because world and existential man are inseparable. Death pertains to being, because it permits the passage of the man who has ceased to exist to the level of pure essence. The drama of death takes place in the depths where the principle-being is hidden; it then emerges from its temple, destroying the walls which separate it from existence. Being is affirmed, and stands ready to become what it is, its intimate faculty of being—that is to say, itself in all its plenitude.

Of course, it is death which makes man a contingent being, because it annihilates men. But in a certain way, it is also the greatest expression of life: it is its apogee. Rather, it is only the existence-being, destined for death, which is contingent, and death is therefore a call to life, because in dying, the being is. Death is awakening, not supreme uncertainty, and even under its law, the being does not become contingent.

How can death be defined? It is the voice of being, manifesting itself in all its potency and reality, because it wishes to see man transformed into what he really is.

4. *The canticle of death*

Death is the *transitus* through which the human being passes, between objective existence and the state of pure essence. Essence then speaks and affirms itself in its creative potency of a new being. Escaping from the trammels of matter, being rises (in the places) without space or time, and assumes its true state of spiritual being, attaining the maximum of its creative force. Death, instead of destroying, confers on the human being power and majesty: it is therefore an episode of life.

And yet, a genius like Goethe, thinking about his imminent end, murmured: "Life is always beautiful." This beauty causes us regrets when we think of losing it: a smiling landscape, a gaze full of beauty and harmony in a human face, an existence, finally. Why so much sadness when we tell ourselves that death will take all of that away? It is because a smile and a glance are something other than human: they are reflections of essence. And that glimpse of beauty is sufficient to cause attachment.

Death has a tragic sense when it represents the rupture of the being and the objective world, for at the moment when man confronts Eternity, he sees drifting away from him all traces of a matter that had perhaps become spiritualized: sounds, lights, spectacles. Man in face of the Being is reduced to a pure state, stripped of everything which could have been seductive for human nature. But it is by losing that he wins back everything, and much more richly than existence had offered it to him.

Despite everything, will man forget that he was a man, existing, material, will being forget that it was human? For life is an uncompleted sonata: what man on his deathbed can say that he has lived enough, that he has completed his life? And if death is not an end, but a continuation, what will man think of his life after death? Will he have the light, distant sensation of a past dream? And will it be a dream identical to those of each night slept on earth?

5. *Potentiality of death*

"Death is no accident," says Heidegger, "it is not something external.... It is our greatest potentiality. Human existence is being-for-the-purpose-of-dying."[1]

But what is potentiality if it does not culminate in the act, in the accomplishment? For the term by definition denotes a faculty, or an uninterrupted force of development within beings. Potentiality and act must therefore normally be combined into a single idea, a single representation. What therefore is the meaning of a potentiality turned toward destruction?

If man's death is the greatest potentiality he possesses, what remains of him? His death becomes the most absurd of absurdities, for death considered as the supreme destiny is the negation of man, the negation of the process leading to the integral human being. True potentiality is pure spirituality, which should neither destroy, nor cease, or at least which ceases as potentiality only when being has been affirmed as spirit and has become pure act. If this were not so, death would be comparable to the potentialities of other human acts, and would really have nothing in common with a unique accomplishment!

Heideggerian thought is too centered on matter to see that the real, unique, exclusive potentiality, the potency which is not lost, is not death, it is spirit, it is the principle-being, inserted into human existence, of which it is the motor element.

---

[1] Quoted in E. Mounier, *Existentialist Philosophies: An Introduction*. Paris: Editions Denoel, 1947, p. 39.

The Dehumanization of Man

1. De-existentialization of man

"In order that God should compel us to die for him," declares Antonio Vieira in his *Sermon for Saint Stephen*, "it was not necessary that Christ should die for us; but it was sufficient that he should be born for us."[1] It is true that the Son of God was born to teach us to die, and to reveal to us that if life is the principle and the means, death (which is the end of existence) is the beginning of a new phase, leading fully to the quality of being. He thus came into the world to "de-existentialize" man, which amounts to a dehumanization. The term does not denote the hardening of the human qualities of spirit or heart: it is simply a question of detaching man from matter, from the world, and especially from himself as something existential, but without ceasing to be human, for "each soul which raises itself raises the world."

It is especially a matter of removing him from his earthly roots, so that, above the human level, he might return to himself; for in this way he will escape the destruction prevailing in the world; or, to strip him of his human habits (which are, however, the *sine qua non* of his existence) and make him reach the heights of spirituality.

The man who wishes to wage that battle to fulfill his being has a

---

[1] *Obras Completas do Padre Antonio Vieira*. Porto (Portugal): Lello e Irmãos, Editores, 1908, p. 233.

weapon, which is faith, but not only that weapon: there is also reason, that force indispensable to "becoming what thou art," for it is the basis of "Know thyself."

2. *The expiatory struggle*

Given the circumstances which surround him and shape him— nature and birth, life and death—man is condemned to struggle. It is an ordeal which is imposed on him by the very fact that he is spirit. His punishment on earth is to discover earths and worlds, penetrate the secrets of matter and life, but at the same time, to plunge into his inner temple in search of his being. This combat is not without hope and is nothing like suicide. For death leads to liberation and culminates in salvation.

But this obligation to fight is no less a drama, in which, moreover, he does not depend on his fellow man, who can do nothing for him and lets him fight alone. Everything depends on his deep desire to conquer, to learn, to advance, to rise, to pray or to create—that is, to use to the fullest the forces available to man in the struggle against the human.

The Principle-Being

1. *The voice of death*

Toward the end of his days, Bergson detected a "metaphysical anguish in the depths of understanding." This complaint seems to echo the *quando consolidabor in te* of St. Augustine. This is the reaction of two men who have heard the voice of death. This voice is a call of being to man; the principle calls on the object it has created and seeks to incorporate it again into itself.

It gives voice to a harmony coming from the depths, the sounds of which do not clearly reach the surface of existence, because only being can intercept them, and when it hears them as its moment of death draws near, it is because it is ready to respond to the invitation of Life.

2. *Man is condemned to be*

To survive destruction, man needs a more solid foundation than mere humanity, which he possesses and which risks being exhausted by the forces of impoverishment at work in the world. But the world is itself a being condemned to disappear, and it is powerless in face of

203

the faculty of being which is within us, as integral human beings. Thus, in order to explain the fact of being in man, to prove that we *are* really, one must not start from existence and from the world, nor from that which suffers the processes of annihilation. It is necessary to find something more, capable of serving as a reference point for everything that, on the surface, tends toward nothingness, and to ascertain that man is condemned to be: a sentence has been pronounced on being, forcing it to be what it is.

Sartre preferred to say that "man is condemned to be free," without giving the reason for such a condemnation, as though it came simply from the fact of existing. But doesn't the obligation to be free in the world correspond, on a smaller scale, to the necessity of being everything that one is, and in particular that characteristic which one possesses so deeply in oneself, the gift of freedom? For before being free in the world, will man not be free within himself?

Neither existence, nor the world, nor freedom will sufficiently explain the obligation imposed on the human being to be human. Only essence, which is its principle and its purpose, provides the elements of a solution.

3. *Music and metaphysics*

In listening to music, do we not feel that there is something undefinable in it? Its strength of expression, which is not intellectual, is nevertheless able to evoke in man a true sense of his being. It directly gives man a notion (undefined, in spite of everything) of his essence, the principle-being.

For there are elements which live in the depths of being; they are essentially substantial, and give man, in a certain way, the forces necessary for his accomplishment. Music in particular can stimulate it; it helps him to think, to pray; it evokes in him the desire for a personal creation, whatever his talent.

And what is our sensation when we listen to music that touches us? That of hearing a kind of call; but a call merely transmitted, for if music is there as an intermediary, it springs in reality from being, inviting us to awaken our spiritual forces: spirituality is tied to art, it is what makes it profound, and creates that emotion which is so powerful that it forces us to ask ourselves, "Is what I feel not the awakening in me of the forces of being?"

Sounds fill the gaps of life, the human gaps: by their warmth, which comes from the depths of being, they can awaken our essence and make us receptive to faith, to divine faith.

4. *Futility of the being without essence*

The being robbed of essence exists only in the disordered imagination of some, in the vision of a blind reason. In reality, it does not exist. It represents precisely and symbolically the frustration of men, their unsatisfied desires, born of the negation of the being which becomes man. This is a desperate state which man reaches when he has been prevented from hearing the voice calling toward real life.

The man without essence, the man without being, is like a garment taken from the body, which it protects, and placed on a dresser. It is something without a reason for being, reduced to mere matter. The being robbed of essence is the imitation of man. It is the man who considers himself simply as existence, and confuses, unconsciously or deliberately, essence and existence. In some human beings, there is an unhealthy tendency to reject what is of pure spirituality in them, that which is most valuable.

Thus, in the man without a soul, nothingness is awakened from its eternal slumber. And that destiny awaits him who denies himself, and renounces ever attaining the integral being? For man without essence is nothingness: he is an eternal condemnation of being.

5. *Questions regarding the act of being*

In order to analyze the act of being, posed by man as a function of his being, several fundamental points must be dealt with. What is being? What is that being capable of possessing in itself such a being? He that is, what is he? And finally, why is man, or, if one wishes, for what reasons is he something in himself?

Heidegger, in *Being and Time*, renews these traditional themes, criticizing the conceptions of Kant and Descartes; he reproaches the German philosopher for having neglected to define being, and for having neglected an ontology of the *Dasein* (or in Kantian terms, an analytical prerequisite to the subjectivity of the subject). But on this point, he brings Kantism back to Cartesianism, by showing that, in Descartes, there is a lack of determination as to the form of being of the *res cogitans* and the meaning of the *sum*: Descartes slid over these points, for he was certain of the *cogito*, not intuitively, but out of fidelity to medieval ontology.

It is interesting, however, to note that Heidegger is much too attached to the "meaning of being" and to its relationship to time and to existence, as though these data were sufficient to make being conceivable, and as though a meaning were assigned to being by the world rather than by the being itself. That is why Heideggerian ontology appears a bit superficial to us.

And his analysis of the relations between being and time do not seem to us to be pushed far enough either. He asks whether time is not "like the horizon of the being," while neglecting to characterize being before time, to define it in itself before putting it into a chronological framework, and in presenting time as a *sine qua non* in the conceptualization of being.

Heidegger further says: "Being is the model of no being, and yet, it touches on every being: its universality is to be sought higher up. Being and its structure are above every being, and every possible determination of a being, which is itself a being. Its transcendence implies the necessity of the most radical individuation." But is this determination really capable, in Heidegger's system, of transcending itself, if one always runs up against existence? Did we not already explain at length the confusion of the existentialists as to the conceptualization of being, because they determine being only on the basis of transient man? And if, finally, Heidegger underlines the need for the most radical individuation, this individuation can depend only on other beings, since every being is unique only by comparison with others. He should rather have tried to find a common basis among all beings. And what is the basis? It is precisely in trying to define it that we will find an answer to the questions about being.

Let us therefore ask, what is this being which *is*—and we answer immediately: it is the human being, destined to attain the fulfillment of the process leading to the perfection of human reality. For being is in all things (since everything is being), but in an imperfect state, and perfection, albeit in relative terms, is attained only by man, although it is quite superior to man and cannot be evaluated by him. The principle-being cannot be observed by human eyes, that is to say, in human terms, for it is that above all which represents human reality.

What is being? From the moment that it *is*, it may be defined as essentially spirit. It is the pure, indestructible essence, which is not reduced in human terms and thus is not destined to become dust. And the essence of which the *ens* or the being of each being consists is the intermediary between man and the Creator.

For man, the fact of being implies his finality, because it is being which gives man the faculty of being; that is, being is the individuating and spiritual vital principle of being called man. If it were not, man would never become a being corresponding to the human model; attached only to existence, man would be a material reality, similar to others, and without his own characteristics: profound individuation, consciousness of self, indestructibility, immortality.

For what reason is being a thing in itself? Because, if it were not, it could not become a man endowed with strength, and would never survive as a man against other men and against all that exists. For man and existence draw their source from an initial force which gives them luminosity, heat, and life, which gives them individuation, which gives them an indefinable something, but which is singular, which would make them be, exist, evolve. Essence and existence can never be considered as separate natures, or as elements superimposed on a single being: both are the being itself which is manifested in a dual way.

6. *Difficulty of defining the principle-being*

The difficulty of defining the principle-being lies in the fact that being transcends the world, and, at the same time, the means of characterization which man possesses, such as the formula, the image, the allegory, are things of the world. Man, as a purely existential being, will therefore never be able either to define or to localize the principle-being, unless he feels it in an extra-material, extra-human way, unless he internalizes it by coming close to his essence and subordinating that which is human in him. But this intimate contact pertains to the ecstatic state, and what man feels when he is transported there he can never express in words. If that sensation or that state were reducible to words, they would lose all their meaning and force. It is therefore perhaps more prudent to limit oneself to sensation.

7. Return to the Cartesian "cogito"

Husserl, in founding phenomenology, exalted Cartesian thought: "Must not the only fruitful renaissance be the one that reawakens the impulse of the Cartesian *Meditations*: not to adopt their content but, in *not* doing so, to renew with greater intensity the radicalness of their spirit?..."[1] But even if, like the German philosopher, we accept that the "Method" aimed at a total reform of philosophy, in order to make of it "a science of absolute foundations," we must see that Descartes, as a man, tried to reach the ego by existential and human means. And he left it to us to define what is the true subject of this return to the ego.

If we speak of the pure *cogito*, that is to say, of the principle-being, we must make sure that the return to it must be done by the being at least tending to be pure, i.e., on the way to its internal temple, and going as far as the boundaries of the human field of vision. It is the opposite of the road traveled by the being when it penetrates materiality, in the existential realm, and becomes man. It is a question of stripping off the existential veils, of stripping off everything that is human in man, for only the being travels, and matter is not permitted to enter those spaces where space and time do not exist.

Neither in Descartes nor in Husserl, then, do we see the pure ego set forth the foundations of metaphysical science. They appear to view it like other sciences, which one can take up without first plunging into essence, for such sciences can be fully attained by existential beings. But the principle-being belongs to pure metaphysics, and it eludes everything that is not the pure integral being.

---

[1]   Edmund Husserl, *Cartesian Meditations*. The Hague: Martinus Nijhoff, 1973, p. 6.

8. *The troubled waters of existentialism*

We do not really know how the existentialists define pure essence, because sometimes they call it freedom, sometimes nature. In any case, they neglect to make a distinction, in the whole of the integral being, between the principle-being and existence. Even in G. Marcel, the conceptualization of being has something troubled and confused about it. By the word "essence," he says, "we may understand the nature of liberty; it is perhaps in my essence as freedom to be able to fit myself or not to my essence as nature. It is perhaps of my essence to be able not to be what I am; in other words, to be able to betray myself. It is not essence as nature which I attain in the thou. Indeed, in addressing him as "him," I reduce the other to pure nature; an animated object which functions in such a way and no other. To the contrary, in addressing the other as thou, I address him, I recognize him as freedom, for he is also freedom and not only nature."

It remains to be seen if I can really conform to my essence as freedom. Will I have that "freedom" which, in the final analysis, is the premeditated destruction of my own freedom? If I do, can I also destroy myself—in the most positive sense of the term—can I, at will, be or cease to be? Or is it possible that I may not be what I am, may nullify in myself the faculty to *be* that death itself cannot suppress?

We must not confuse essence with freedom or nature; rather, it is necessary to radically distinguish what essence represents from what existence represents for the integral being: yet even when G. Marcel speaks of essence, we do not know exactly if he is referring to it or to existence. Thus, in the thought "It is perhaps of my essence to be able not to be what I am," he seems to believe that I can even stifle the freedom in myself, or deprive myself of it, without clearly stating that I cannot destroy my faculty to be free. For man carries out the act of being for reasons that are beyond his grasp, and he is inexorably condemned to be, as we have so often stated.

If I suffer this condemnation, I am my being, and cannot be eliminated either by time or by the world or by matter or by other men. I am my being by virtue of myself, and I cannot doubt it, or doubt the principle-being, without dragging myself through empty voids which even the darknesses of the cosmos cannot suggest. Reason itself, which does not know, because it is impotent, the reasons for creation, rebels against such an annihilation, and, even though limited, it dares to reject a system which envisions such a possibility.

For it would mean calling into question all the reasons God had for creating us; God's privileged creature need not fear suffering the fate of dead matter.

9. *Answer to the question, "What am I?"*

The existentialists assure us that any answer to the question, "What am I?" comes from man. G. Marcel, for example, writes: "What qualification have I to resolve this question? And consequently, any answer to it *from me* should be revoked in doubt. Can someone else provide me with it?... The qualification which that other person may have to answer me, the possible validity of his statement, is perceived by me.... I cannot, therefore, refer without contradiction to anything but an absolute judgment, but one that at the same time would be more internal to me than my own."[1] G. Marcel considers that he has not encountered this type of judgment.

We, on the other hand, believe that if the question comes from the surface, that is, from man, the answer comes from inside, for it is our being which answers. Man merely recognizes a truth (for example, that he is a being, that he is something, that he is a being or something else imagined during his search for himself, but never that he is nothing). Very well, this "something" we call *being*, and we say that the answer which is heard comes from it. To doubt it would be to doubt oneself as human, because, even if we wish to, we cannot deny the essence of ourselves.

As for that "something other than me, but more internal to me than myself," it is perhaps the principle-being which is manifested by a voice providing the spiritual liaison with the man-being, because man as existence is not only existence, and cannot totally detach himself from his principle. If it is true that the answer given by man to the question "What am I?" loses its value because of the fact that it comes from him, the objection falls once it is shown that the answer does not come from man, but that it springs from the depths of being, and that it is the principle-being which solves the problem.

---

[2] *Journal Métaphysique*. Paris: Editions Aubier Montaigne, 1935, p. 181.

Despair and Life

1. *Dual aspect of despair*

Despair springs from the depths of being; it is a pain felt inside man, especially stinging, often, in that it appears less on the surface. For it is being that causes suffering, and suffering thus does not touch other people. But being itself does not suffer, it is man who despairs of the search for himself, for his principle, for his lost being. Being does not despair, it remains eagerness, emanation, an invitation to man lost in the entrails of the world or in himself.

Despair is the sign of man's march toward his being, despite the impossibility of reaching the regions of his essence in this way; it is the encounter or approximation of the infinite and the finite in the whole of the integral being. It is also a sign that being aspires, with an irrepressible desire, to its own liberation, but at the same time regrets not manifesting itself in the world, especially when man is not going toward it, but remains deaf and without faith.

Briefly, it is everything that prevents essence from touching existence, and, in the opposite sense, everything that prevents man from coming close to his principle, to his own being.

2. *True life*

True life is the life of the being. It is lived only by those who are seeking to come close to it. Existential life is a visible manifestation which man is incapable of transcending, because the means at his disposal are human, fallible, and because he lives in this materiality without being able to escape from it.

To do so, it would be necessary for him to plunge within himself, to depersonalize himself, dehumanize himself, even though existential life is more obvious, almost irrefutable. Yet the life of being is more real, more profound, it has a greater meaning, even if one cannot fully enjoy it, and it can only be attained fully through death. For the life of being is not exactly "a life"; there are no vital signs in it. However, there are no words to define it, and we must use the vocabulary of man. What is lived by being can be felt only imperfectly by existential man.

3. *Dialectic of being and of incarnation*

Incarnation is not the fundamental fact of being. It would be, rather, of man, i.e., for the being as existence in the world. Of the essence-being, incarnation represents only the means by which it is fully realized. Incarnation is closely tied to existence, because man exists only as an incarnate being, even in order to manifest his will and his consciousness, those two transcendental realities which provided, one to Maine de Biran, the other to Descartes, the basis of their *cogito*.

Yet one would say, rather, that G. Marcel based his on the life of the body, forgetting that the flesh decays and cannot provide anything eternal. For us, the living person of the existential being is something too ephemeral to serve as a principle for a universal system. The sole transcendental element in man is his essence, for it is pure spirit. Gilson may have discovered this truth if he had followed his thought to the end. But he is satisfied to ask the question, without answering it: "What is the act by virtue of which that which *is* exists?"[1]

As for Bergson, the essence which he sees in man he calls duration, and he calls that which develops and makes being grow in the being "creative evolution."

In any case, no one asks himself what there is prior to essence, for this would be to seek the true reason for being of creation. However,

---

[1] Etienne Gilson, *El Ser y la Esencia*. Buenos Aires: Desclée de Brouwer, 1951, p. 18.

let us ask: What is the act by which that which is, is? It is the divine breath. But why seek to discover an act of that nature, since it escapes our understanding? Let us therefore begin our search with the fact of being, which man cannot doubt, even in the midst of the drama of existence.

4. *Dialectic of being and of man*

Man—or more exactly, the being providing his humanity and exercising his human faculty—is existence. He is by definition existence in the world. But the being which becomes man *was*, prior to existence, and it is only continuing to be. Even if it *is* solely in man, it already was what it is before taking human shape, in the world where it was existentialized.

Even though it is prior to man, being is what it is by using man, or in other words, it is man who exercises the faculty of being which his being gives him. And that is why being is the quality peculiar to man. Being, man, existence are the three degrees in the scale of the same being, of the integral being where the principle is: essence-being, the course; existence, the earthly end; man-being, the absolute end; the return to oneself through death (which gives the being the plenitude of being).

In certain respects, therefore, man is more than human, for in the being which precedes man, in the being which becomes man, essence precedes existence and prevails over man himself, and the reason for this is that existential life is the accomplished being. Hence the majesty of man and his immortality especially, a quality that is not given to him as anyone, but as pure being, that same pure being which was already man before.

That is why it is strange that this characteristic of a being without limits, infinite, inexhaustible, has been attributed by some to "time"! On the one hand, since time is nothing, one cannot say that it is about to end: only the real ends! But time ceases with the death of each person, because, necessarily, each individual limits his universe to himself. Only the integral man outlasts man, the world and death.

5. *Poetry and being*

Whereas poetry, in Proust's opinion, is transfigured vision, but always rooted in the real, man's glance toward his interior is a vision of the immaterial.

The vision of being is essentially spiritual, too spiritual to have a foundation in any objective reality. Its object is unreal, or rather antireal, the opposite of a materialized thing: it is situated beyond the limits of existence, in a different atmosphere, in the regions of the unknowable.

Harmfulness of Existentialism

The Negation of Reason

1. *Existentialism and materialism*

Existentialism opened horizons for philosophy, expanded its human content, and brought to light problems never before dealt with. But it sins by excess: it exaggerates the existential aspect of man, and makes existence the substratum of the integral human being, in such a way as to reduce reason to impotence. But reason is a manifestation of being. Without deifying it, as the rationalists of the 18th century did, we must demand that it not be destroyed. On the other hand, existentialism exalts time, that enigmatic notion which constitutes the neuralgic point of the philosophies of Bergson and Heidegger (the former renewed the concept; the latter spatialized it, taking away its destructive character).

In making existence the basis of their system, many contemporary thinkers have taught a philosophy of life which tends to scorn thought and to reject the idea of essence. They thus materialize man, some of them unconsciously, because they call themselves Christians without seeing that the primacy of life and of existence over being leave no more room for the soul.

J. Huizinga tried to reconcile existential experience with thought. But behind it, he should have placed the being which thinks, and not have been satisfied to reproach the existentialists for a point of departure too close to materialism. "It is thus," he says, "that the anti-Noetian forces of an entire century united to form a powerful current that would soon threaten to burst the spiritual dikes of the culture, which were deemed to be unshakable. It was Georges Sorel who, in *Réflexions sur la violence*, drew from all this the practical and political consequences which they imply, thus becoming the spiritual father of all contemporary dictatorships."[1]

Thus, albeit only indirectly, existentialism is an evil: it leads to despising the essence of the human being, the being which *is* because it is spirit, and to deifying in its place, by a philosophical attitude precisely comparable to that which led to the building of altars to Reason, existence and life. It is still the idolatry of a human entity! But to despise being, without even destroying it, but relegating it to a secondary level, is to reduce man to his apparent size, to deny that he is a giant, and to deliver him up to the good will of forces that flow from the world. Separated from his foundations, man can only lose himself, and the goddess Existence will not save him.

The materialist wave which has surged forward during these last two centuries has affected the heart of being and threatens to choke it. But man's true reaction should not be Nietzschean; rather, he should plunge within himself. There he will find a light which fortifies him and which will enable him to once again climb the ladder which leads to life, to existence and to the world.

2. *Decadences and dawns*

Among the causes of the decay of the Roman Empire, J. Huizinga lists: weakening of the political system and the foreign invasion; the slowdown of economic activity; the spread of a form of religion which destroyed the ancient cults, taking the command of social life away from the pagan cadres.

Is the modern world at that point? The economy, although relatively dynamic, remains subject to explosions of which the 1929 crisis

---

[1]   J. Huizinga, *Incertitudes*. Paris: Librairie de Médicis, 1939, p. 107.

gave us an example; Christianity hardly risks being replaced by another religion (for it is undeniably the highest of the spiritual doctrines), but it is threatened by the atheism which has invaded the West; as for the political-social system of the atomic era, it is dominated by the struggle between the elite and the mass, which has made it lose much of its effectiveness.

It is necessary, therefore, to build a new road, and to create a philosophy which aggrandizes not life, existence, or reason, but being and spirit, and which tends to elevate man, in this difficult period of history. A job that must be done by man himself, in order to dehumanize and de-existentialize himself. Only a philosophy of the superiority of being over man could help the world regain its lost equilibrium.

Moreover, a spiritualism seems little by little to be dawning on the horizons of the current era, allowing us to hope that new men will emerge who will move history forward by pulling humanity from the slumber into which it is plunged. Being seems to awaken in the world, but it knows that it is not a thing of this world, and that it is its own entity which came from another universe.

3. *Renaissance of being?*

Our era is that of freedom, which bursts forth on the surface of the globe and comes from the depths of hearts, irresistibly; but this freedom germinated in the depth of being.

Thus, if man dies so that another can emerge, the one which has replaced him must say farewell to an already vanished world. The new era is the era of being. But it will begin only when the man of today has regained his lost being.

Let humanity, therefore, throw itself into the search for its being!